Modern C for Absolute Beginners

A Friendly Introduction to the C Programming Language

Second Edition

Slobodan Dmitrović

Apress®

Modern C for Absolute Beginners: A Friendly Introduction to the C Programming Language, Second Edition

Slobodan Dmitrović
Belgrade, Serbia

ISBN-13 (pbk): 979-8-8688-0223-2
https://doi.org/10.1007/979-8-8688-0224-9

ISBN-13 (electronic): 979-8-8688-0224-9

Managing Director, Apress Media LLC: Welmoed Spahr
Acquisitions Editor: Melissa Duffy
Development Editor: James Markham
Coordinating Editor: Gryffin Winkler

Cover designed by eStudioCalamar

Cover image by Noel_Bauza on pixabay (pixabay.com)

Distributed to the book trade worldwide by Apress Media, LLC, 1 New York Plaza, New York, NY 10004, U.S.A. Phone 1-800-SPRINGER, fax (201) 348-4505, e-mail orders-ny@springer-sbm.com, or visit www.springeronline.com. Apress Media, LLC is a California LLC and the sole member (owner) is Springer Science + Business Media Finance Inc (SSBM Finance Inc). SSBM Finance Inc is a **Delaware** corporation.

For information on translations, please e-mail booktranslations@springernature.com; for reprint, paperback, or audio rights, please e-mail bookpermissions@springernature.com.

Apress titles may be purchased in bulk for academic, corporate, or promotional use. eBook versions and licenses are also available for most titles. For more information, reference our Print and eBook Bulk Sales web page at http://www.apress.com/bulk-sales.

Any source code or other supplementary material referenced by the author in this book is available to readers on GitHub (https://github.com/Apress). For more detailed information, please visit https://www.apress.com/gp/services/source-code.

Paper in this product is recyclable

For Sanja and Katarina

Table of Contents

About the Author

Slobodan Dmitrović is a software consultant, trainer, and author of several programming books. He is a professional R&D software developer with two decades of experience in the industry. Slobodan provides C and C++ training courses to corporate clients and academic institutions. Contact Slobodan at `linkedin.com/in/slobodan-dmitrovic`.

About the Technical Reviewer

German Gonzalez-Morris is a polyglot software architect/ engineer with 20+ years in the field, with knowledge in Java, Spring Boot, C/C++, Julia, Python, Haskell, and JavaScript, among others. He works with cloud (architecture), web-distributed applications, and microservices. German loves math puzzles (including reading Knuth, proud of solving some of Don's puzzles), swimming, and table tennis. Also, he has reviewed several books, including an application container book (WebLogic) and some on languages (C, Java, Spring, Python, Haskell, TypeScript, WebAssembly, Math for coders, regexp, Julia, data structures and algorithms). You can see details in his blog `https://devwebcl.blogspot.com/` or X/Twitter account: `@devwebcl`.

Acknowledgments

I want to thank the readers, friends, and peers who have supported me in writing the second edition of this book.

I am indebted to Peter Dunne, Glenn Dufke, Bruce McGee, Tim Crouse, Jens Fudge, Rainer Grimm, and Rob Machin for all their work, help, and support.

I am grateful to the outstanding professionals at Apress who have supported me throughout the writing process.

I am thankful to all the amazing software developers, architects, and entrepreneurs I met and collaborated with.

Introduction

Dear reader, congratulations on choosing to learn the C programming language, and thank you for picking up this book. My name is Slobodan Dmitrović, and I will try to introduce you to the wonderful world of C programming to the best of my abilities.

This book is divided into five parts. In Part 1, we cover the C language basics. Part 2 explains the C standard library, and Part 3 introduces us to modern C standards. Part 4 explains the dos and don'ts in modern C. The final part consists of the Appendices. Let us get started!

PART I

The C Programming Language

CHAPTER 1

Introduction

1.1 What Is C?

C is a programming language – a general-purpose, procedural, compiled programming language. C language was created by Dennis Ritchie in the late 1960s and early 1970s. The C program is a collection of C source code spread across one or more source and header files. Source files, by convention, have the *.c* extension, and header files have the *.h* extension. Source and header files are plain text files that contain some C code.

1.2 What Is C Used For?

C is often used for the so-called *systems programming*, which is operating systems programming, application programming, and embedded systems programming, to name a few. A large portion of Linux and Windows operating systems was programmed using C. C is often used as a replacement for an assembly language. C language constructs efficiently translate to the hardware itself.

1.3 C Compilers

To compile and run a C program, we need a C compiler. A compiler compiles a C program and turns the source code into an object file. The linker then links the object files together and produces an executable or library. For the most part, we say we *compile* the program and assume the compilation process results in an executable file we can run. At the time of writing, some of the more popular C compilers are

- gcc – As part of the GCC toolchain
- Clang – As part of the LLVM toolchain

3

© Slobodan Dmitrović 2024
S. Dmitrović, *Modern C for Absolute Beginners*, https://doi.org/10.1007/979-8-8688-0224-9_1

- Visual C/C++ compiler – As part of the Visual Studio IDE

- MinGW – A Windows port of the GCC

1.3.1 Installing Compilers

Here, we describe how to install C compilers on Linux and Windows and how to compile and run our programs.

1.3.1.1 On Linux

To install a GCC compiler on Linux, open a terminal window and type:

```
sudo apt install build-essential
```

This command installs a GCC toolchain, which we can use to compile, debug, and run our C programs. Using a text editor of our choice, let us create a file with the following code:

```
#include <stdio.h>

int main(void)
{
    printf("Hello World!\n");
}
```

Let us save this file as a *source.c*. To compile this program using the GCC compiler, we type:

```
gcc source.c
```

This will produce an executable file with a default name of *a.out*. To run this file, type the following in a console window:

```
./a.out
```

Running this program should output the `Hello World!` text to our console window.

Note   The preceding example code is for demonstration purposes. For now, let us take the source code inside the *source.c* file for granted. We will get into detailed code explanation and analysis in later sections.

To install a clang compiler on our Linux system, type:

```
sudo apt install clang
```

This command installs another compiler called *Clang*, which we can also use to compile our programs. To compile our previous program using a clang compiler, we type:

```
clang source.c
```

As before, the compiler compiles the source file and produces an executable file with the default name of *a.out*. To run this executable file, we type:

```
./a.out
```

The compiler choice is a matter of preference. Just substitute gcc with clang and vice versa. To compile with warnings enabled, type:

```
gcc -Wall source.c
```

Warnings are not errors. They are messages indicating that something in our program might lead to errors. We want to eliminate or minimize the warnings as well.

To produce a custom executable name, add the -o flag, followed by the custom executable name so that our compilation string now looks like:

```
gcc -Wall source.c -o myexe
```

To run the executable file, we now type:

```
./myexe
```

The ISO C standard governs the C programming language. There are different versions of the C standard. We can target a specific C standard by adding the -std= flag, followed by a standard name such as c99, c11, c17, and c2x (for the upcoming c23 standard). To compile for a C99 standard, for example, we would write:

```
gcc -std=c99 -Wall source.c
```

To compile for a C11 standard, we use:

```
gcc -std=c11 -Wall source.c
```

To compile for an upcoming C23 standard, we type:

```
gcc -std=c2x -Wall source.c
```

If we want to adhere to strict C standard rules, we add the -pedantic compilation flag. This flag issues warnings if our code does not comply with the strict C standard rules. Some of the use cases are:

```
gcc -std=c99 -Wall -pedantic source.c
gcc -std=c11 -Wall -pedantic source.c
gcc -std=c17 -Wall -pedantic source.c
gcc -std=c2x -Wall -pedantic source.c #currently used for the C23 standard
```

To compile and run the program using a single statement, we type:

```
gcc source.c && ./a.out
```

This statement compiles the program and, if the compilation succeeds, executes the *a.out* file.

Let us combine it and use the following compilation strings in our future projects. If using gcc, we write:

```
gcc -Wall -std=c11 -pedantic source.c && ./a.out
```

If using Clang, we write:

```
clang -Wall -std=c11 -pedantic source.c && ./a.out
```

1.3.1.2 On Windows

On Windows, we can install *Visual Studio*. Choose the *Create a new project* option, make sure the *C++* option is selected, choose *Empty Project*, and click *Next*. Enter the project and solution names or leave the default values and click *Create*. We have now created an empty Visual Studio project. In the *Solution Explorer* window, right-click on a project name and choose *Add – New Item…*. Ensure the *Visual C++* tab is selected, click the *C++ File (.cpp)* option, modify the file name to *source.c*, and click *Add*. We can use a different file name, but the extension should be *.c*. Double-click the *source.c* file and paste our previous *Hello World* source code into it. Press *F5* to run the program. To compile for the C11 standard, use the `/std:c11` compiler switch. To compile for the C17 standard, use the `/std:c17` compiler switch. Currently, Visual Studio supports C standards up to C17.

Alternatively, install the MinGW (Minimalist GNU for Windows) and use the compiler in a console window, as we would on Linux.

So far, we have learned how to set up the programming environments on Linux and Windows and compile and run our C programs. We are now ready to start with the C theory and examples.

1.4 C Standards

The C programming language is a standardized language. There were different C standards throughout history. The first notable standard was the ANSI C, and now it is the ISO standard known as the ISO/IEC:9989 standard. Some of the C standards throughout the years are as follows:

- **ANSI C** standard (referred to as ANSI C and C89)

- **C90** (official name: ISO/IEC 9899:1990, it is the ANSI C standard adopted by ISO; the C89 and C90 are the same things)

- **C99** (ISO/IEC 9899:1999)

- **C11** (ISO/IEC 9899:2011)

- **C17** (ISO/IEC 9899:2018)

- The upcoming standard, informally named **C23** (the formal name will probably become ISO/IEC 9899:2024)

CHAPTER 2

Our First Program

This chapter describes the main program entry point, how to work with comments, and how to write a simple *"Hello World"* program.

2.1 Function main( )

Every C program that produces an executable file must have a starting point. This starting point is the function main(). The function main is the function that gets called when we start our executable file. It is the program's main entry point. The signature of the function main is:

```
int main(void) {}
```

The function main is of type int, which stands for integer, followed by the reserved name main, followed by an empty list of parameters inside the parentheses (void). The name void inside the parentheses means the function accepts no parameters. Following is the function body marked with braces {}. The opening brace { marks the beginning of a code block, and the closing brace } marks the end of the code block. We write our C code inside the code block marked by these braces. The code we write there executes when we start our executable file.

For readability reasons, we can put braces on new lines:

```
int main(void)
{

}
```

We can keep the opening brace on the same line with the main function definition and have the ending brace on a new line:

```
int main(void) {

}
```

© Slobodan Dmitrović 2024
S. Dmitrović, *Modern C for Absolute Beginners*, https://doi.org/10.1007/979-8-8688-0224-9_2

Note   Braces placement position is a matter of conventions, preferences, and coding styles.

In early C standards, the function `main` was required to have a `return 0;` statement. This statement ends the program and returns the control to the operating system. The return value of 0 means the program finished the execution as expected. It ended normally. If the `main` function returns any value other than 0, it means the program ended unexpectedly. So, in previous standards, our blank program would look like:

```c
int main(void)
{
    return 0;
}
```

Statements in C end with a semicolon `;`. The `return 0;` statement within the `main` function *is no longer required* in modern C. We can omit that statement. When the program execution reaches the closing brace, the effect is the same as if we explicitly wrote the statement. In modern standards, we can simply write:

```c
int main(void)
{

}
```

We often see the use of the following, also valid `main` signature:

```c
int main()
{
    return 0;
}
```

While this signature indicates there are no parameters, in ANSI C, it could potentially allow us to call the function with any number of parameters. Since we want to avoid that, we will be using the `int main(void)` signature, which explicitly states the function does not accept parameters.

With that in mind, we will be using the following `main` skeleton to write our code throughout the book:

```c
int main(void)
{

}
```

Note   There is another main signature accepting two parameters: int
main(int argc, char* argv[]). We will describe it later in the book when
we learn about arrays, pointers, and command-line arguments.

2.2 Comments

We can have comments in our C program. A comment is a text that is useful to us but
is ignored by the compiler. Comments are used to document the source code, serve as
notes, or comment out the part of the source code.

A C-style comment starts with /* characters and ends with */ characters. The
comment text is placed between these characters. Example:

```c
int main(void)
{
    /* This is a comment in C */
}
```

The comment can also be a multi-line comment:

```c
int main(void)
{
    /* This is a
    multi-line comment in C */
}
```

Starting with C99, we can write a single-line comment that starts with a double slash
// followed by a comment text:

```c
int main(void)
{
    // This is a comment
}
```

We can have multiple single-line comments on separate lines:

```
int main(void)
{
    // This is a comment
    // This is another comment
}
```

Comments starting with the double slash // are also referred to as *C++-style comments*.

2.3 Hello World

Let us write a simple program that outputs a "Hello World" message in the console window and explain what each line of code does. The full listing is:

```
#include <stdio.h>

int main(void)
{
    printf("Hello World!");
}
```

The first line #include <stdio.h> uses the #include preprocessor macro to include the content of the <stdio.h> header file into our source.c file. The standard-library header file name stdio.h is surrounded with matching <> parentheses. This standard-library header is needed to use the printf() function. We call this function inside the main function body using the following blueprint:

```
printf("Message we want to output");
```

The printf function accepts an argument inside the parentheses (). In our case, this argument is a *string constant* or a *character string* "Hello World!". The string text is surrounded by double quotes"". The entire printf("Hello World!") function call then ends with the semicolon ; and then we call it a *statement*. Statements end with a semicolon in C. Macros such as the #include <stdio.h> do not end with a semicolon.

We can output text on multiple lines. To do that, we need to output a new-line character, which is \n. Example:

```c
#include <stdio.h>

int main(void)
{
    printf("Hello World!\nThis is a new line!");
}
```

Output:

```
Hello World!
```

We can split the text into two printf function calls for readability reasons. Remember, each time we want the text to start on a new line, we need to output the new-line character \n:

```c
#include <stdio.h>

int main(void)
{
    printf("Hello World!\n");
    printf("This is a new line!");
}
```

Output:

```
Hello World!
This is a new line!
```

This has the same effect as if we placed a new-line character at the beginning of the second printf function call:

```c
#include <stdio.h>

int main(void)
{
    printf("Hello World!");
```

```
    printf("\nThis is a new line!");
}
```

Output:

```
Hello World!
This is a new line!
```

CHAPTER 3

Types and Declarations

In this chapter, we will learn about the built-in types in C and variable declarations.

3.1 Declarations

A *declaration* declares a (variable) name. When we declare a variable, we specify its type and variable name, and the compiler reserves memory for our variable. This occupied space is called an *object* or *data object* in memory. These data objects are accessed by names we call *variables*. We need to declare a variable before we can use it. To declare a variable, we put the `type_name` before the `variable_name` and end the entire statement with a semicolon `;`. The declaration pseudo-code looks like this:

```
type_name variable_name;
```

We can declare multiple variables of the same type by separating them with a comma:

```
type_name variable_name1, variable_name2, variable_name3;
```

Variable names can contain both letters and numbers but must not start with a number. C is a case-sensitive language, so `myvar` and `MyVar` are two different, independent names. Variable names should not start with underscore characters as in `_myvar` or `__myvar`.

3.2 Introduction

What is a *type*? A type is a property that describes a range of values and allowed operations on those values. An instance of a type is called an *object* or a *data object*. When we declare a variable, we are creating an instance.

© Slobodan Dmitrović 2024
S. Dmitrović, *Modern C for Absolute Beginners*, https://doi.org/10.1007/979-8-8688-0224-9_3

There are different built-in types in C. For example, one type can hold (store) characters, another type can hold whole numbers, and some other type can be used to store floating-point values. Some of the built-in types are

- char – Holds character values

- int – Holds whole numbers

- float – Holds floating-point values of single precision

- double – Holds floating-point values of double precision

Our program data is stored in computer memory. Computer memory is an array of memory cells called *bits*. A bit can have two states we symbolically refer to as 1 and 0. A group of 8 bits is often called a *byte*. A byte of memory has its own label/number, which we call an *address*.

We can visualize a byte as a rectangular area, an occupied space in memory with its address. This address is a number, often represented by a hexadecimal number:

Figure 3-1. *A single byte with an address*

Types have different sizes. Data represented by variables of different types occupy a different amount of bytes in memory. For example, type char is *one* byte in size. We say that it is *one byte long* and can be used to store a single character. Other types have different sizes. For example, type int can be 4 bytes in size.

There are *lower* and *upper limits* to values each type can hold, a minimum or maximum value a type can store.

There are special *qualifiers* we can apply to the preceding types, such as *long* and *unsigned*. We discuss each type in more detail in the following sections.

3.3 Character Type

Type char allows us to store a single character. To declare a single variable of type char inside the main function body, we write:

```
int main(void)
{
    char mychar;
}
```

The statement char mychar; is a *variable declaration*. In simple words: *from now on, there will be a* char *variable called* mychar. We also say that mychar *is of* char *type*.

The variable declared inside the function main is also called a *local variable*. It is local to the main function. Local variables are not initialized by default and contain random values. Once declared, we can access the variable. For example, we can assign a value to it using an assignment operator:

```
int main(void)
{
    char mychar;
    mychar = 'a';
}
```

The first line inside the main function body declares a variable, and the second line assigns it a value of 'a'. We used a character constant 'a' to assign a value to our variable using the = assignment operator. Character constants are enclosed in single quotes ''. Examples of character constants are 'a', 'A', and 'z'. Some character constants must be *escaped* using the backslash character \. Some of the escape-sequence characters are

- The *new-line character* '\n'

- A *single quote character* '\''

- A *double quote character* '\"'

- A *tab character* '\t'

The character type char is also an integral type. We can say it is a small integer. In type char, every character constant is represented by a matching number inside the *encoding table*. This encoding table is called a *character set*, and it might be ASCII or some other table, depending on the implementation. For example, the preceding character constant 'a' is represented by a number 97 in the ASCII table. So, we can assign a value of 97 to our mychar variable, and the underlying byte value would be the same:

```
int main(void)
{
    char mychar;
    mychar = 97;
}
```

It represents the same byte value using different constants, either by using a character constant 'a' or an integer constant 97. For the most part, we will use character constants to assign values to char variables.

We can also think of type char as being a small integer type.

Instead of declaring a variable and then assigning a value to it, we could *initialize* the variable:

```
int main(void)
{
    char mychar = 97;
}
```

To print out our variable's value, we will use the printf function. To print out a single variable value, we call the printf function using the following syntax:

```
printf("%format_specifier", variable_name);
```

If we want to print out multiple variables, we will use the multiple format specifiers/placeholders in the double quotes, followed by a comma-separated list of variables:

```
printf("%format_specifier1 %format_specifier2", variable_name1,
variable_name2);
```

The %format_specifier1 part is a placeholder and a format specifier for the value of variable_name1. The format specifier specifies how our variable should be formatted/interpreted when we send it to the output/console window. The %format_specifier2 is a placeholder for the value of variable_name2, and so on. The format specifier is also called a *conversion specifier*.

To print out the character variable as an actual character, we can use the c format specifier:

```
#include <stdio.h>

int main(void)
{
      char mychar;
      mychar = 'a';
      printf("%c", mychar);
}
```

Output:

```
a
```

Explanation: The printf() function writes data to the *standard output*, which is our console window. The printf function can accept multiple arguments. The first argument is the double-quoted text. Inside the double-quoted text, there is a placeholder for our variable. This placeholder consists of a starting percentage sign **%** followed by the *format specifier*, which in our case is **c**. There are different format specifiers for different types. These determine how the value of our variable is to be presented/printed within the quoted text.

To print out the character variable value as an integral number, we use the %d or the %i format specifier:

```
#include <stdio.h>

int main(void)
{
      char mychar;
      mychar = 'a';
      printf("%d", mychar);
}
```

Output:

The size of the type char is one byte. This means that mychar occupies exactly one byte of memory storage. We can check the size of the object by using the sizeof operator. The sizeof operator returns the object's or type's size in bytes:

```
#include <stdio.h>

int main(void)
{
    char mychar;
    mychar = 'a';
    printf("The size of a character object is %zu byte(s).",
    sizeof(mychar));
}
```

Output:

```
The size of a character object is 1 byte(s).
```

The %zu format specifier is used for the return type of the sizeof operator. The char type range varies depending on the implementation but is usually between -128 and +127.

A special unsigned qualifier can be applied to integral types, including type char. This qualifier means the type can hold only positive values and a zero. The size in memory remains one byte, but now the type can hold twice as many positive values. The maximum value of an unsigned char is usually 255. Example:

```
#include <stdio.h>

int main(void)
{
    unsigned char mychar = 255;
    printf("The value of mychar is: %d", mychar);
}
```

Output:

```
The value of mychar is: 255
```

A fair amount of theory surrounds even a simple thing such as the char type, but we need not worry. Each section is accompanied by plenty of source code examples and exercises.

3.4 Integer Type

The integer type, int, is used to store whole (integral) numbers/values and perform certain operations on them. To declare an integer variable, we write int variable_name;. Let us write a program that declares an integer variable and assigns a value to it:

```
int main(void)
{
    int x;
    x = 123;
}
```

There are different *integer constants* we can assign to int variables.

The first kind is the *decimal integer constant* represented by negative and positive numbers, for example, -256, 0, 128, etc. The second kind is the *octal constant*. Octal constants begin with a zero sign of 0, followed by numbers from 0 to 7. An example of an octal constant is 012, equal to a decimal value of 10. The third kind is a *hexadecimal constant*. This constant begins with 0x or 0X, followed by symbols from 0 to 9 and letters from A to F. The hexadecimal value of 0xA represents a decimal number of 10. Let us write a program that assigns a value of 10 to three different integer variables using decimal, octal, and hexadecimal notation:

```
int main(void)
{
    int x;
    x = 10;  // decimal constant
    int y;
    y = 012; // octal constant
    int z;
    z = 0xA; // hexadecimal constant
}
```

In this example, both x, y, and z have the same value of 10 (ten), represented by three different constants. All these constants are of type int.

We can print the integer value using different format specifiers, %d for decimal, %o for octal, and %x or %X for hexadecimal representation:

```
#include <stdio.h>

int main(void)
{
    int x;
    x = 10;
    printf("Decimal: %d Octal: %o Hexadecimal: %X", x, x, x);
}
```

Output:

```
Decimal: 10 Octal: 12 Hexadecimal: A
```

Here, we print out the same value but with three different representations.

Depending on the hardware and the implementation, the type int is usually 4 bytes wide in memory. It can hold values from at least −32768 to +32767, but on our computer, this range is generally from -2147483648 to +2147483647.

Some *modifiers* or *qualifiers* can be applied to type int. They are signed, unsigned, short, and long. Integers are *signed* by default, so instead of saying signed int, we simply write int. The unsigned qualifier says the type int can only hold positive values and a zero. The size of the type is the same. Unsigned integers can now hold twice as many positive numbers as the regular (signed) int.

An example of unsigned int is:

```
#include <stdio.h>

int main(void)
{
    unsigned int x = 123456789u;
    printf("The value of an unsigned integer is: %u", x);
}
```

Output:

The value of an unsigned integer is: 123456789

We can rewrite the preceding example so that the int part is omitted:

```
#include <stdio.h>

int main(void)
{
    unsigned x = 123456789u;
    printf("The value of an unsigned integer is: %u", x);
}
```

Output:

The value of an unsigned integer is: 123456789

Note   When using any of these specifiers on type int, we can omit the int part and write only the specifier(s) name(s).

The unsigned integer constants have u or U suffix, such as our 123456789u value. We used the %u specifier to print out the value of an unsigned integer.

Other specifiers that can be applied are short and long. These specifiers change the length of the integer type. Type short is often 2 bytes in length and long is at least 4 bytes in length. Here is a source code example demonstrating the use of short and long types:

```
#include <stdio.h>

int main(void)
{
    short x;
    x = 1234;
    printf("The value of a short integer is: %d\n", x);
```

```
    long y;
    y = 1234567891;
    printf("The value of a long integer is: %ld\n", y);
}
```

Output:

```
The value of a short integer is: 1234
The value of a long integer is: 123456789
```

The first part declares a short integer x and prints its value using the %d format. The \n after the %d placeholder is just a new-line character, and it is not part of the specifier. The second part declares a long integer y. Long integer constants have the l or L suffix, such as our 1234567891 value. We used the %ld format to print out the value of a long integer.

These type specifiers can be chained together so that we can have an unsigned short:

```
#include <stdio.h>

int main(void)
{
    unsigned short x;
    x = 1234u;
    printf("The value of an unsigned short integer is: %hu\n", x);
}
```

Output:

```
The value of an unsigned short integer is: 1234
```

Here, we used the %hu format specifier to format and print out the value of an unsigned short. Our 1234u constant also has the u suffix as it is of unsigned type. There is no specific suffix for a short type.

To declare and print out the unsigned long value, we write:

```
#include <stdio.h>

int main(void)
{
    unsigned long y;
    y = 123456789ul;
    printf("The value of an unsigned long variable is: %lu\n", y);
}
```

Output:

```
The value of an unsigned long variable is: 123456789
```

We used the %lu format to print out the value of an unsigned long. Notice that our 123456789ul constant now carries both u and l suffixes since it is of unsigned long type.

Starting with the C99 standard, there is also a long long integer type that is at least 8 bytes long. Its constants have the ll or LL suffixes. To print out the value of the long long type, we use the %lld or %lli format specifier:

```
#include <stdio.h>

int main(void)
{
    long long x;
    x = 12345678911;
    printf("The value of a long long integer is: %lld", x);
}
```

Remember to compile for at least the C99, C11, C17, or the C23 standard, using the following command-line compilation strings:

```
gcc -Wall -std=c99 -pedantic source.c && ./a.out
```

or:

```
gcc -Wall -std=c11 -pedantic source.c && ./a.out
```

From C99 onward, there can also be an unsigned long long type. Its constants carry the ull, ULL, llu, or LLU suffixes. We use the %llu format specifier to print out the value:

```
#include <stdio.h>

int main(void)
{
    unsigned long long x;
    x = 123456789llu;
    printf("The value of an unsigned long long integer is: %llu", x);
}
```

3.5 Floating-Point Types

There are three types for representing floating-point numbers. The first is called float, the second type is called double, and the third type is called long double.

3.5.1 float

Type float is a type used for storing single-precision floating-point numbers. The type is 4 bytes wide. Floating-point numbers are also called *real numbers*. In a floating-type number such as 123.456, there is the *whole number part* (123), the *decimal separator* (.), and the *fractional/decimal* part 456. To declare a variable of type float, we write:

```
int main(void)
{
    float myfloat;
    myfloat = 123.456f;
}
```

We will describe two floating-point constants used to represent floating-point values. The *floating-point constant*, such as the 123.456f, carries a suffix f or F, which makes it of type float. The same value represented by an *exponent constant* has the form 123456e-3f. It means *123456 times 10 to the power of -3*. To represent a number 100 using an exponent constant, we would write 1e2f. To represent a value of 0.123 using a decimal constant, we can also write .123 without the leading 0.

To print out a value of type float, we use the %f format specifier:

```
#include <stdio.h>

int main(void)
{
    float myfloat;
    myfloat = 123.456f;
    printf("The value of a floating-point variable is: %f", myfloat);
}
```

Output:

```
The value of a floating-point variable is: 123.456001
```

This example prints out the value of 123.456001 because the default precision of a %f format specifier is 6, so it also adds the (imprecise) 001 part. To print out only the three decimal places, we use the %.3f format:

```
#include <stdio.h>

int main(void)
{
    float myfloat;
    myfloat = 123.456f;
    printf("The value of a floating-point variable is: %.3f", myfloat);
}
```

The output is now 123.456 because the %.3f specifier uses three positions (characters/places) to display the floating-point value's fractional part. We can also explicitly specify the whole and fractional parts' lengths using the %3.3f format specifier.

3.5.2 double

Another type for storing floating-point values is type double. It is 8 bytes wide and offers increased precision and range as compared to type float. To declare a variable of type double, we write:

```
int main(void)
{
    double d;
    d = 123.456;
}
```

Floating-point constants without suffixes, such as our `123.456`, are of type `double` by default. So, for a simple decimal constant of type `double`, we write `123.456`, and for an exponent constant, we write `123456e-3`.

To print out the value of type `double`, we use the `%f` or the `%lf` format specifier inside the `printf` function:

```
#include <stdio.h>

int main(void)
{
    double mydouble;
    mydouble = 123.456;
    printf("The value of a double variable is: %.3f", mydouble);
}
```

Output:

```
The value of a double variable is: 123.456
```

When to use `float` and when to use `double`? It depends on the context, the hardware, and our needs. Float occupies less memory than `double`, might be faster than `double`, but is less precise. When increased precision is required, we can opt for `double`.

In general, we should prefer `double` to `float`.

3.5.3 long double

The third floating type is called a `long double`. The type has increased precision and range. To declare a variable of this type, we write:

```
int main(void)
{
    long double mylongdouble;
    mylongdouble = 123456.789l;
}
```

Long double constants have l or L suffixes. To print out the value of a long double, we use the %Lf format specifier:

```
#include <stdio.h>

int main(void)
{
    long double mylongdouble;
    mylongdouble = 123456.789l;
    printf("The value of a long double variable is: %.3Lf",
    mylongdouble);
}
```

Output:

```
The value of a long double variable is: 123456.789
```

29

CHAPTER 4

Exercises

4.1 Hello World with Comments

Let us write a program that has comments in it and outputs a "Hello World!" message on one line and "C rocks!" on a new line:

```c
#include <stdio.h>

int main(void)
{
    // this is a comment
    /* This is an
    multi-line comment */
    printf("Hello World.\n");
    printf("C rocks!.\n");
}
```

Output:

```
Hello World.
C rocks!.
```

© Slobodan Dmitrović 2024
S. Dmitrović, *Modern C for Absolute Beginners*, https://doi.org/10.1007/979-8-8688-0224-9_4

4.1.1 Declaration

Write a program that declares four variables of type char, int, float, and double, respectively:

```
int main(void)
{
    char c;
    int x;
    float f;
    double d;
}
```

4.1.2 Definition

Write a program that declares and initializes four variables of type char, int, float, and double, respectively:

```
int main(void)
{
    char c = 'a';
    int x = 123;
    float f = 123.456f;
    double d = 789.101112;
}
```

4.1.3 Outputting Values

Write a program that initializes and prints four variables of type char, int, float, and double, respectively:

```
#include <stdio.h>

int main(void)
{
    char c = 'a';
    int x = 123;
    float f = 123.456f;
```

```
    double d = 789.101112;
    printf("%c\n", c);
    printf("%d\n", x);
    printf("%f\n", f);
    printf("%f\n", d);
}
```

Output:

```
a
123
123.456001
789.101112
```

CHAPTER 5

Operators

Operators are an essential part of the language. This chapter explains what they are and how they are used. It might seem that there is plenty of theory surrounding this subject but do not worry. We need to adopt the theoretical part to use it in practical code examples later in the book.

5.1 Introduction

What is the operator? An operator is a language entity that performs/applies an operation to its arguments and returns a result. One or more different symbols are used to represent operators. To better understand the terminology, let us look at a simple mathematical expression: x + y. Here, + is an *operator*. It applies an addition operation using x and y. Here, x and y are called *operands*, where x is a *left operand* and y is the *right operand*. The entire x + y part is called an *expression*.

Depending on the type of operation, we can have different categories of operators. Some of them are *arithmetic, relational, assignment, logical, bitwise*, and other operators.

5.2 Arithmetic Operators

Arithmetic operators perform arithmetic operations on their arguments. Arithmetic operators are

- + – Addition
- - – Subtraction
- * – Multiplication
- / – Division
- % – Modulo

© Slobodan Dmitrović 2024
S. Dmitrović, *Modern C for Absolute Beginners*, https://doi.org/10.1007/979-8-8688-0224-9_5

The *addition operator* + allows us to add the operands together. The subtraction allows us to subtract y from x. The multiplication operator multiplies the x and y, and the division operator divides x with y.

The division can be an *integer division* or a *floating-point division*. The integral division occurs when both operands are of some integral type, such as int. The result of such division is the whole number only, and the remainder (the decimal part) is discarded. For example, the result of the 9 / 2 expression is 4, and the fractional part of .5 is discarded. Since both 9 and 2 are of type int, the result of the entire expression is also of type int. If only one operand is of the floating-point type, the entire expression is of the floating-point type. For example, the result of 9.0 / 2 is 4.5 as at least one of the operands is of a floating-point type.

Let us look at what the % modulo operator does. It returns the remainder of the integral division. The result of the x % y expression is the remainder of the x / y integral division. For example, the result of the 9 % 2 is equal to 1. The result of an integral division 9 / 2 is equal to 4, as the fractional part gets discarded. And 4 * 2 is equal to 8. When we subtract 8 from 9, we get the modulo result equal to 1 in our case.

The precedence of *, /, and % operators is higher than the + and – operators. In an expression like x + y * z, the subexpression y * z is evaluated first. The x + (the result of the y * z subexpression) is evaluated next.

5.3 Assignment Operator

The assignment operator = assigns a value to the variable/expression. A source code example of a simple assignment operator would be:

```
#include <stdio.h>

int main(void)
{
    int x;
    x = 123;
    printf("%d", x);
}
```

In an x = 123 expression, the value of 123 gets assigned to variable x. In this expression, everything occurring on the left side of the assignment operator = is called a *left-hand side* expression or *lhs* for short. In our case, it is a simple variable x. And everything occurring on the right of the assignment operator is called a *right-hand side* expression or *rhs* for short, which in this example is an integer constant 123. We say that the assignment operator *assigns a value of rhs to lhs*. In our case, it assigns a value of 123 to our variable x. We can also assign the value of one variable to another:

```c
#include <stdio.h>

int main(void)
{
    int x;
    int y;
    x = 123;
    y = x;
    printf("%d", y);
}
```

In a y = x; statement, we assigned the value of x to y. In a y = x expression, we only assign the copy of the *value* of x to y, not the memory address. The two data objects x and y are two different data objects in memory. Changing the value of either one does not affect the value of the other one.

Let us use the assignment operator to assign values to variables of different types such as char, int, and float:

```c
#include <stdio.h>

int main(void)
{
    char c;
    c = 'A';
    int x;
    x = 123;
    float f;
```

```
    f = 123.456f;
    printf("Char: %c int: %d float: %.3f", c, x, f);
}
```

Here, we declare the variables, assign the values of constants to our variables, and then print them. We used three different types, constants, and format specifiers.

5.4 Compound Assignment Operators

Compound assignment performs binary operation on both operands and then assigns the value to its left-hand side operand. Some of the compound assignments are +=, -=, *=, /=, and %=.

The compound assignment operator += in the x += 123 expression is equivalent to x = x + 123. Example:

```
#include <stdio.h>

int main(void)
{
    int x = 0;
    x += 123;
    printf("%d", x);
}
```

To use a *= compound assignment operator, we would need to initialize x to 1 as we use the multiplication inside the compound statement operator:

```
#include <stdio.h>

int main(void)
{
    int x = 1;
    x *= 123;
    printf("%d", x);
}
```

As before, the x *= 123; statement is a shorter way of writing the x = x * 123; statement.

5.5 Relational Operators

Relational operators compare the values of two operands/expressions. They are

- \> – Greater than
- \< – Less than
- \>= – Greater than or equal to
- \<= – Less than or equal to

In an expression x < y, we check if x is less than y. If that is true, the entire x < y expression gets the value 1, which stands for *true*. If x is not less than y, the entire expression is evaluated to 0, which is *false*. Example:

```c
#include <stdio.h>

int main(void)
{
    int x = 123;
    int y = 456;
    int islessthan = x < y;
    int isgreaterthan = x > y;
    printf("The value of \"is less than\" expression is: %d\n",
    islessthan);
    printf("The value of \"is greater than\" expression is: %d\n",
    isgreaterthan);
}
```

Output:

```
The value of "is less than" expression is: 1
The value of "is greater than" expression is: 0
```

5.6 Equality Operators

There are two kinds of equality operators:

- == – Equal to

- != – Not equal to

In an x == y expression, we check if (the value of) x equals y. If that is the case, the entire x == y expression gets the value of 1, which stands for true. If not, the expression gets the value of 0, which means false. In an x != y expression, we check if x is *not equal* to y. If true, the expression is evaluated to 1; else, it gets the value of 0. Example:

```
#include <stdio.h>

int main(void)
{
    int x = 123;
    int y = 456;
    int isequalto = x == y;
    int isnotequalto = x != y;
    printf("The value of the \"is equal to\" expression is: %d\n",
    isequalto);
    printf("The value of the \"is not equal\" to expression is: %d\n",
    isnotequalto);
}
```

Output:

```
The value of the "is equal to" expression is: 0
The value of the "is not equal" to expression is: 1
```

Let us explain what the "*entire x == y expression gets the value of 1 or 0*" means. It means expressions themselves are of a certain type, and they hold values.

These expressions are often used as *conditions* in the so-called *conditional statement*. Their value is inspected. If the expression evaluates to 1, the condition is *true*; if it evaluates to 0, the condition is *false*. We cover these topics in more detail later in the book when we discuss the *if-statement*.

5.7 Logical Operators

The logical operators perform logical (bool/Boolean) operations on their operands and return the result of such operations. The logical operators are

- && – Logical AND operator

- || – Logical OR operator

- ! – Unary negation operator

The logical operator && performs the logical AND operation on its operands and returns the value of 1 when both operands are 1. In all other cases, it returns a value of 0.

The logical operator || performs the logical OR operation and returns 0 when both operands are 0. In all other cases, it evaluates the expression to 1. The unary negation operator ! performs the *negation operation* on its only right-hand side operand. So 0 becomes 1, and 1 or any other nonzero value becomes 0.

Example:

```
#include <stdio.h>

int main(void)
{
    int x = 1;
    int y = 0;
    int myand = x && y;
    int myor = x || y;
    int mynegation = !x;
    printf("The value of an AND expression is: %d\n", myand);
    printf("The value of an OR expression is: %d\n", myor);
    printf("The value of a NEGATION expression is: %d\n", mynegation);
}
```

Output:

```
The value of an AND expression is: 0
The value of an OR expression is: 1
The value of a NEGATION expression is: 0
```

5.8 Increment and Decrement Operators

Increment operator ++ is used to add 1 to a variable, and decrement operator -- is used to subtract 1 from a variable.

Both these operators can be used in their so-called *prefix* or *postfix* forms. When used before the variable name, as in ++my_var or --my_var, they are called *prefix operators*. When they are used after the variable name, as in my_var++ or my_var--, they are called *postfix operators*. We now have four possible combinations:

- ++var_name – prefix ++ operator

- var_name++ – postfix ++ operator

- --var_name – prefix -- operator

- var_name-- – postfix -- operator

The prefix operator increments/decrements the value of a variable before the variable is used in an expression. When used as a postfix operator, the program evaluates a variable in an expression and then increments its value.

A simple example:

```c
#include <stdio.h>

int main(void)
{
    int x = 10;
    int y = 10;
    int myprefix = ++x;
    int mypostfix = y++;
    printf("The prefix result: %d, the postfix result: %d\n", myprefix,
    mypostfix);
}
```

Output:

```
The prefix result: 11, the postfix result: 10
```

Explanation: We have two `int` variables, x and y, both having a value of `10`. We use the prefix ++ operator on x. The x is incremented by 1 before the result of an expression is assigned to `myprefix` variable. Then, we use a postfix operator on y. The result of an expression is assigned to `mypostfix` var, and then the value is incremented by one.

Increment and decrement operators increment/decrement a variable value by 1 and save us from typing the: `my_var = myvar + 1` or `my_var = myvar - 1`.

Note   Whether we use a *prefix* or a *postfix* form is relevant only in the context of the **current** *expression/statement* where these operators are used. By the time the program flow reaches the `printf` point, both x and y will have the value of `11`.

There are also other kinds of operators, which we explain later in the book, as we learn further and adopt new things.

5.9 Operator Precedence

Some operators have higher precedence than others. For example, operators / and * have higher precedence over operators + and -. This is also true in the science of math. For example, in an expression `x + y * z`, the `y * z` part/subexpression gets evaluated first. Then, this subexpression result gets added to x, as the * operator has higher precedence over the + operator.

If we need the `x + y` subexpression to be evaluated first, we surround the subexpression with parentheses ( ):

`(x + y) * z`

This forces the `x + y` subexpression to be evaluated first. Then, the result of this subexpression gets multiplied by z. This is because the ( ) operator has higher precedence over the + and * operators. The ( ) operator groups the items together.

Here is the list of some of the operators sorted by precedence, from higher to lower:

++ -- – Postfix increment and decrement

() – Function call operator

[] – Array subscript

. – Structure member access

-> – Structure member access through a pointer

++ -- – Prefix increment and decrement

+ - – Unary plus and minus

! – Logical NOT

(type_name) – Cast operator

* – Dereference operator

& – Address-of

* / % – Multiplication, division, and modulo

+ - – Addition and subtraction

<< >> – Bitwise left shift and right shift

< <= – Relational operators

> >= – Relational operators

== != – Equality operators

&& – Logical AND

|| – Logical OR

?: – Ternary conditional operator

= – Assignment operator

+= -= – Compound assignments

CHAPTER 6

Expressions

What is an *expression*? An expression is operators and operands grouped together to perform some calculations and yield a result. There are different kinds of expressions. There are *arithmetic expressions*, as in x + y; *comparison expressions*, as in x > y; *assignment expressions*, as in x = y; and *logical expressions*, such as x && y.

An expression can consist of multiple *subexpressions*, as in z = x + y. Here, the x + y can be treated as an *arithmetic subexpression* inside the *assignment expression*.

The entire expression is of a particular type. What that type is depends on the nature of the result of the entire expression. For example, if we had a simple expression x + y, and x and y were of type int, then the entire expression would be of type int too. But what if one operand was of type double and the other was of type int? What would the expression result/type be? The result would be double as the int operand is *promoted* to type double. In general, *smaller/narrower* types are converted to *wider* types in arithmetic expressions. For example, char becomes int, float, or a double, depending on the second operand type.

6.1 Initialization

We can declare a variable and assign a value to it on the same line. This approach is called *initialization*. We say we *initialize* the variable to a certain value. The blueprint for the initialization is:

```
type_name variable_name = some_value;
```

Initialization example:

```
#include <stdio.h>

int main(void)
{
```

© Slobodan Dmitrović 2024
S. Dmitrović, *Modern C for Absolute Beginners*, https://doi.org/10.1007/979-8-8688-0224-9_6

```
    char c = 'a';
    int x = 123;
    float f = 123.456f;
    double d = 789.123;
    printf("The values are: %c, %d, %.3f, %.3f\n", c, x, f, d);
}
```

Output:

```
The values are: a, 123, 123.456, 789.123
```

This example initializes and prints out several different variables using appropriate format specifiers. If we only declare and do not initialize those variables, they would hold random garbage values.

Having some_type myvar; is called *declaration,* and having some_type myvar = some_value; is called *initialization* or *definition.* Initialization (definition) is also a declaration.

Tip   It is a good practice to always initialize your variables before using them.

6.2 Type Conversion

Expressions of one type can be converted to expressions of another type. Some conversions are implicit and occur automatically. We can also *explicitly* convert an expression to a certain type using the (convert_to_type)expression syntax. A simple example where we *explicitly* convert the type char to type int:

```
#include <stdio.h>

int main(void)
{
    char c = 'A';
    int x;
    x = (int)c;
    printf("The result is: %d\n", x);
}
```

The following example relies on implicit conversion from int to double:

```
#include <stdio.h>

int main(void)
{
    int x = 10;
    int y = 30;
    double d = x / y;
    printf("The result is: %f\n", d);
}
```

Output:

```
The result is: 0.000000
```

The result of an integer division is implicitly converted to type double, and we get the value of 0.000000. Suppose we explicitly cast the first operand x to double. In that case, we get the expected result of a floating-point division, which is 0.333333. Example:

```
#include <stdio.h>

int main(void)
{
    int x = 10;
    int y = 30;
    double d = (double)x / y;
    printf("The result is: %f\n", d);
}
```

Output:

```
The result is: 0.333333
```

Alternatively, we can make at least one of the operands of type double, and the whole expression will be of type double, as the other operand of type int gets automatically promoted into a type double when the x / y expression is evaluated. This is also called an integer promotion. Example:

```c
#include <stdio.h>

int main(void)
{
    double x = 10.0;
    int y = 30;
    double d = x / y; // y here gets promoted to type double, because x
    is of type double
    printf("The result is: %f\n", d);
}
```

Output:

```
The result is: 0.333333
```

CHAPTER 7

Statements

This chapter explains statements in general – expressions ending with a semicolon (;) and statements built into the language itself.

7.1 Introduction

What is a *statement*? A statement is an expression ending with a semicolon symbol (;). For example, x + y is an *expression*, but x + y; is a *statement*. Let us list a few simple statements we have used so far:

- int x; – A statement containing a declaration
- int x = 123; – A statement containing an initialization
- x = 123; – A simple assignment statement
- z = x + y; – A statement with multiple expressions
- x++; – A statement having a postfix increment expression
- printf("Hello World!"); – A function call statement

Every statement except the last one is called an *expression statement* because they consist solely of *expressions*. The last statement is a *function call statement*. We often say that statements are *executed* and expressions are *evaluated*.

Let us write a simple source code example to explain the terminology:

```
#include <stdio.h>

int main(void)
{
    int x = 123;
    int y = 456;
```

© Slobodan Dmitrović 2024
S. Dmitrović, *Modern C for Absolute Beginners*, https://doi.org/10.1007/979-8-8688-0224-9_7

```
    int z = x + y;
    printf("The result is: %d\n", z);
}
```

Output:

```
The result is: 579
```

In this example, statements inside the function main() are executed in a *sequence,* one after the other. Statements inside the function body marked with { } are also called *compound statements.* The entire block is often referred to as a *block of statements* or code block.

Note   There is no semicolon sign after the right brace } marking the end of a code block.

Now, with the terminology out of the way, let us learn about the *built-in statements.* These statements are part of the C programming language itself. They have reserved names and special syntax and can be divided into several categories:

Selection statements (conditional statements):

- if statement
- if-else statement
- switch statement

Iteration statements or loops:

- for statement
- while statement
- do-while statement

7.2 Selection Statements

Selection statements execute other statements based on some expression (condition). If that expression evaluates to anything other than 0, they proceed to execute other statements. Here, we will explain the following selection statements:

- `if` statement
- `if-else` statement
- `switch` statement

7.2.1 if

The `if` statement is of the following syntax:

```
if (some_condition)
    some_statement;
```

The `if` statement checks an expression (a condition) first. The condition is surrounded by parentheses (). If that condition (expression) evaluates to true (anything other than 0), the specified statement is executed. If the condition is false (the condition evaluates to 0), the statement will not be executed.

The following example uses an `if` statement to execute a single `printf` statement:

```
#include <stdio.h>

int main(void)
{
    int x = 123;
    if (x < 150)
        printf("The x is less than 150.\n");
}
```

The `if` statement checks the condition first. In our case, it checks if x is less than some arbitrary number 150. If so, the condition is true, and the `printf` statement is executed. If the condition is false, the `printf` call will not be executed.

The `if` statement can also execute a block of statements/multiple statements marked with braces {}. The syntax is:

```
if (some_condition)
{
      some_statement_1;
      some_statement_2;
      some_statement_3;
      // ...
}
```

An example that uses the if statement to execute a block of statements:

```
#include <stdio.h>

int main(void)
{
      int x = 123;
      if (x < 150)
      {
            printf("The x is less than 150.\n");
            printf("This is a second statement.\n");
      }
}
```

Output:

```
The x is less than 150.
This is a second statement.
```

The if statement is a perfect use case for logical operators && and || where these operators can appear as part of the condition expression. An example that uses the logical AND operator &&:

```
#include <stdio.h>

int main(void)
{
      int x = 123;
      int y = 456;
      if (x < 150 && y > 150)
```

```
    {
        printf("The condition is true.\n");
    }
}
```

   Output:

```
The condition is true.
```

The condition in this `if` statement says: If **both** *x is less than 150* **and** *y is greater than 150*, the entire condition is true, and the `printf` statement gets executed. Let us now write a similar example that uses a logical OR operator || instead:

```
#include <stdio.h>

int main(void)
{
    int x = 123;
    int y = 456;
    if (x < 150 || y > 150)
    {
        printf("The condition is true.\n");
    }
}
```

   Output:

```
The condition is true.
```

This condition checks if **either** x is less than 150 **or** y is greater than 150. If **either** of these is true, the entire expression is true, and the `printf` function gets called/executed inside the code block.

   To use a negation operator ! inside the `if` statement condition, we write:

```
#include <stdio.h>

int main(void)
{
```

```
    int x = 0;
    if (!x)
    {
            printf("The condition is true.\n");
    }
}
```

Output:

```
The condition is true.
```

In this example, the negation operator ! negates the value of x. Since x was 0, the negation operator turns it into 1, which stands for true, rendering the entire !x expression true. Since now the condition is true, the if statement executes the code block with our printf function in it.

Note   It is a good practice always to use the code block marked with {} inside the **if** and other conditional statements, even when the code block contains only one statement. This is for readability reasons.

7.2.2 if-else

In addition to an if statement, there is also an if-else variation. The if-else statement is of the following syntax:

```
if (some_condition)
        some_statement_1;
else
        some_statement_2;
```

The if-else statement checks the condition value, and if the condition is true, it executes some_statement1. If the condition is false, it executes some_statement_2 coming after the else keyword. Example:

```
#include <stdio.h>
int main(void)
{
      int x = 123;
      if (x < 150)
            printf("The condition is true. X is less than 150.\n");
      else
            printf("The condition is false. X is not less than 150.\n");
}
```

Output:

```
The condition is true. X is less than 150.
```

This example uses a simple condition to check if x is less than some arbitrary number 150. If the condition is true, the first printf function executes. Otherwise, when x is not less than 150 (when the condition is false), the second printf statement executes.

To execute more than one statement in either if or else sections, we surround the statements with code blocks {}:

```
#include <stdio.h>

int main(void)
{
      int x = 123;
      if (x < 150)
      {
            printf("The condition is true. X is less than 150.\n");
            printf("This is the second statement in the if-block.\n");
      }
      else
      {
            printf("The condition is false. X is not less than 150.\n");
            printf("This is the second statement in the else-block.\n");
      }
}
```

Output:

```
The condition is true. X is less than 150.
This is the second statement in the if-block.
```

As before, when executing statement(s) from conditional statements, it is a good practice to use the code blocks {}, even if there is only one statement to be executed:

```c
#include <stdio.h>

int main(void)
{
    int x = 123;
    if (x < 150)
    {
        printf("The condition is true. X is less than 150.\n");
    }
    else
    {
        printf("The condition is false. X is not less than 150.\n");
    }
}
```

Output:

```
The condition is true. X is less than 150.
```

7.2.3 switch

The switch statement executes a code based on the integral expression value. It is of the following syntax:

```c
switch (expression)
{
    case value_1:
        statements;
        break;
```

```
    case value_2:
        statements;
        break;
    case value_3:
        statements;
        break;
    default:
        statement;
        break;
}
```

The preceding code is a switch statement blueprint. Let us break the preceding wordy syntax into pseudo-code segments and analyze the switch statement structure, one segment at a time.

The switch statement evaluates the value of an expression inside parentheses followed by a switch statement body marked with {}. The expression inside parentheses must be of type char, int, signed, unsigned, or enum (we cover enums later in the book). So far, it looks like the following:

```
switch (expression)
{
}
```

The switch statement body can have one or more case: labels. Each case label has a *constant expression* that is of char, int, signed, unsigned, or enum type followed by a colon sign (:). Now the switch statement looks like this:

```
switch (expression)
{
    case value_1:
    case value_2:
    case value_3:
}
```

If the constant-expression value inside the `case:` label matches the value of the expression, the statement inside that `case` label is executed. The statement needs to be followed by a `break;` statement. A `break` or `return` statement exits the `switch` statement. If we leave out the `break;` statement, the code would fall through, meaning the code in the next case label would also execute. Now, our switch statement looks like:

```
switch (expression)
{
    case value_1:
        some_statement;
        break;
    case value_2:
        some_statement;
        break;
    case value_3:
        some_statement;
        break;
}
```

And finally, there is a `default:` label. If none of the case label values match the expression value, the statement inside the `default:` label gets executed. It is good practice to put a `break` statement inside the `default` label as well. Our full pseudo-code switch statement now looks like:

```
switch (expression)
{
    case value_1:
        statements;
        break;
    case value_2:
        statements;
        break;
    default:
        statement;
        break;
}
```

Now, we are ready to write a complete source code example that uses the switch statement:

```c
#include <stdio.h>

int main(void)
{
    int x = 123;
    switch (x)
    {
    case 100:
        printf("The value of x is 100.\n");
        break;
    case 123:
        printf("The value of x is 123.\n");
        break;
    case 456:
        printf("The value of x is 456.\n");
        break;
    default:
        printf("None of the above values matches the value of x.\n");
        break;
    }
}
```

Output:

```
The value of x is 123.
```

This example initializes an integer variable x to the value of 123. Then, it uses the switch statement to check if the value of x is equal to either 100, 123, or 456. Since the second case label indeed checks for the value of 123, the printf statement in that label is executed.

Let us now write an example that uses the type char:

```c
#include <stdio.h>

int main(void)
{
        char c = 'a';
        switch (c)
        {
        case 'a':
                printf("The value of c is 'a'.\n");
                break;
        case 'b':
                printf("The value of c is 'b'.\n");
                break;
        case 'c':
                printf("The value of c is 'c'.\n");
                break;
        default:
                printf("None of the above values matches the value of c.\n");
                break;
        }
}
```

Output:

```
The value of c is 'a'.
```

We initialize a char variable to the value of 'a'. The switch statement checks for matching value and executes the code in the appropriate case label. We are now using the type char. This means the constant expressions inside the case labels can now use *character constants* marked with single quotes ' '. Here, the value inside the first case label matches the value of the variable c, and the statement inside this label is executed.

We use the switch statement when we want to check for multiple values and then act accordingly. The switch statement is equivalent to having multiple if branches.

7.3 Iteration Statements

Iteration statements allow us to execute other statements multiple times/repeatedly. These statements are also called *loops*. There are three different loops in C:

- while loop

- do-while loop

- for loop

7.3.1 while

The while statement is of the following syntax:

```
while(some_expression)
{
    some_statements;
}
```

The while statement executes one or more statements, while the expression inside the parentheses is true/not equal to 0. A simple example that prints out a message five times:

```
#include <stdio.h>

int main(void)
{
    int mycounter = 0;
    while (mycounter < 5)
    {
        printf("Hello World from a while loop.\n");
        mycounter++;
    }
}
```

Explanation: We initialize a variable that represents a counter to a value of 0. The while statement evaluates the expression mycounter < 5 inside the parentheses. If the expression is true/other than 0, the while loop executes the code inside the while loop body. This process repeats until the mycounter < 5 becomes false/0.

In this example, there are two statements inside the while loop body. The first statement prints out a simple message, and the second statement mycounter++; increases the counter by one. At some point, the mycounter will get the value of 5, causing the condition mycounter < 5 to become 0 and the while statement to end. In general, the while loop may execute 0 or more times as its condition is at the beginning.

7.3.2 do-while

The do-while statement is of the following syntax:

```
do
{
    some_statements;
} while (some_expression);
```

The do-while loop continues to execute statements until the condition/expression while the condition is true/ other than 0. In different words, it repeatedly executes a code block until the condition becomes equal to 0/false. The do-while statement is guaranteed to execute the statements inside its body *at least once*. This is because the condition is placed at the end, after the do-while code block. Let us write an example that uses a do-while loop to display a message five times:

```
#include <stdio.h>

int main(void)
{
    int mycounter = 0;
    do
    {
        printf("Hello World from a do-while loop.\n");
        mycounter++;
    } while (mycounter < 5);
}
```

Explanation: The example initializes the integer variable to 0. Then the do-while code block executes the printf and the mycounter++ statements. Then it checks the condition mycounter < 5. If the condition evaluates to anything other than 0, the code inside the code block is executed again. Once the mycounter reaches the value of 5, the condition mycounter < 5 evaluates to 0 and the do-while loop exits.

7.3.3 for

The for loop has the following blueprint:

```
for (initialization; condition; iteration;)
{
    // loop body
}
```

The for loop repeatedly executes the statements in its loop body as long as the *condition* is true. In addition to a condition, the for loop also has its *initialization* and *iteration* parts.

The for loop initializes a counter variable in the initialization part, checks the condition, executes the loop body, and then increments or decrements the counter in the iteration part. The loop continues to execute the statements in the loop body as long as the condition is true.

In plain words, the for loop is like a while loop but with its own *counter*, a *condition*, and an *iteration* part. Let us write an example that prints out a message five times:

```
#include <stdio.h>

int main(void)
{
    for (int i = 0; i < 5; i++)
    {
        printf("Hello World from a for loop.\n");
    }
}
```

Explanation: In the for loop section, we declare an integer variable called I and initialize it to 0. This variable will serve as our counter, and this expression is evaluated only once. Next, the condition i < 5 is evaluated. If it evaluates to true/other than 0, the statement in the for loop body is executed. Then, the i variable is incremented by one in the i++; part. Now, the entire process (except the initialization part) repeats itself. When i reaches 5, the condition i < 5 evaluates to 0, and the for loop exits.

To execute a loop body ten times, we would rewrite the condition to i < 10, and so on. The counter can also use the prefix variation in the iteration segment:

```
#include <stdio.h>

int main(void)
{
    for (int i = 0; i < 5; ++i)
    {
        printf("Hello World from a for loop.\n");
    }
}
```

To print out the value of a counter, we write:

```
#include <stdio.h>

int main(void)
{
    for (int i = 0; i < 5; i++)
    {
        printf("Counter value: %d\n", i);
    }
}
```

The type of the counter variable i can also be size_t (which stands for unsigned integer type), unsigned and similar.

The counter itself does not have to start from 0, it can start from any number. It is zero by convention. for loops are often used to print out array elements which themselves are indexed from 0. We will cover this in more detail when we learn about *arrays* and *array indexes*.

In a nutshell, the for loop is a convenient way to repeatedly execute statements a given (fixed) number of times while having access to an index/counter. One example is iterating over array elements. We discuss this topic in the following chapters.

CHAPTER 8

Exercises

8.1 Arithmetic Operations

Write a program that initializes two int numbers. Declare a third int variable that represents the sum of the previous two integers. Print out the result:

```c
#include <stdio.h>

int main(void)
{
    int x = 123;
    int y = 456;
    int z = x + y;
    printf("The result is: %d\n", z);
}
```

Output:

```
The result is: 579
```

8.2 Integral Division

Write a program that performs an integer division:

```c
#include <stdio.h>

int main(void)
{
    int x = 9;
    int y = 2;
```

© Slobodan Dmitrović 2024
S. Dmitrović, *Modern C for Absolute Beginners*, https://doi.org/10.1007/979-8-8688-0224-9_8

```
    int z = x / y;
    printf("The result is: %d\n", z);
}
```

Output:

```
The result is: 4
```

8.3 Floating-Point Division and Casting

Write a program that performs a floating-point division using integral operands. Cast one of the operands to type double to obtain a floating-point result:

```
#include <stdio.h>

int main(void)
{
    int x = 9;
    int y = 2;
    double z = (double)x / y;
    printf("The result is: %.3f\n", z);
}
```

Output:

```
The result is: 4.500
```

8.4 Equality Operator

Write a program that checks if two integer variables are of the same value.

```
#include <stdio.h>

int main(void)
{
    int x = 10;
    int y = 20;
```

```
    if (x == y)
    {
            printf("The values are equal.\n");
    }
    else
    {
            printf("The values are not equal.\n");
    }
}
```

Output:

```
The values are not equal.
```

8.5 Relational and Logical Operators

Write a program that checks if an integer variable is greater than 50 and less than 100.

```
#include <stdio.h>
int main(void)
{
    int x = 75;
    if (x > 50 && x < 100)
    {
            printf("The value is greater than 50 and less than 100.\n");
    }
    else
    {
            printf("The value is not within the (50..100) range.\n");
    }
}
```

Output:

```
The value is greater than 50 and less than 100.
```

8.6 The switch Statement

Write a program that defines a simple integer variable with a value of 2. Use the switch statement to check if the value is inside the [1..3] range:

```
#include <stdio.h>

int main(void)
{
    int x = 2;
    switch (x)
    {
    case 1:
        printf("The value is equal to 1.\n");
        break;
    case 2:
        printf("The value is equal to 2.\n");
        break;
    case 3:
        printf("The value is equal to 3.\n");
        break;
    default:
        printf("The value is not inside the [1..3] range.\n");
        break;
    }
}
```

Output:

```
The value is equal to 2.
```

8.7 Iteration Statements

Write a program that increments and prints out an integer variable ten times using a for loop and a while loop:

```c
#include <stdio.h>

int main(void)
{
    printf("Using a for-loop:\n");
    for (int i = 0; i < 10; i++)
    {
        printf("%d ", i);
    }
    printf("\nUsing a while-loop:\n");
    int counter = 0;
    while (counter < 10)
    {
        printf("%d ", counter);
        counter++;
    }
}
```

Output:

```
Using a for loop:
0 1 2 3 4 5 6 7 8 9
Using a while loop:
0 1 2 3 4 5 6 7 8 9
```

CHAPTER 9

Arrays

What is an array? An array is one or more data objects of the same type positioned next to each other in memory. Once declared, the array size is fixed we cannot add nor remove elements to and from the array. The array itself is also a type.

9.1 Declaration

An array is a sequence of (one or more) elements of a certain type. To declare an array, we use the following syntax:

```
type_name array_name[array_size];
```

To declare an array of five integers, we write:

```
int main(void)
{
    int myarr[5];
}
```

The number 5 in the square brackets [ ] says how many array elements there are. We declared an array of five elements in our example, so the compiler reserves the space in memory for five integers.

To declare an array of, for example, five floats, we would write:

```
int main(void)
{
    float myarr[5];
}
```

Array elements are indexed. The first array element has an index of 0, and the last array element has an index of *number_of_elements - 1*.

© Slobodan Dmitrović 2024
S. Dmitrović, *Modern C for Absolute Beginners*, https://doi.org/10.1007/979-8-8688-0224-9_9

9.2 Subscript Operator

Individual array elements are accessed using a subscript operator [ ] and an index. To access the first array element, we write myarr[0]. To access the second array element, we write myarr[1]. Using this operator, we can assign values to each array element. Example:

```
int main(void)
{
        int myarr[5];
        myarr[0] = 10;
        myarr[1] = 20;
        myarr[2] = 30;
        myarr[3] = 40;
        myarr[4] = 50;
}
```

To print out the entire array, we can use a for loop and a subscript operator []:

```
#include <stdio.h>

int main(void)
{
        int myarr[5];
        myarr[0] = 10;
        myarr[1] = 20;
        myarr[2] = 30;
        myarr[3] = 40;
        myarr[4] = 50;
        for (int i = 0; i < 5; i++)
        {
                printf("%d ", myarr[i]);
        }
}
```

Output:

---

10 20 30 40 50

In this example, we used a for loop to go through the entire array and print out the individual array elements. The loop has a counter i that goes from 0 to 4. We use this variable as an index inside the subscript operator [i] to access and print out individual array elements with myarr[i].

Let us now print out both the array indexes and array values:

```c
#include <stdio.h>

int main(void)
{
    int myarr[5];
    myarr[0] = 10;
    myarr[1] = 20;
    myarr[2] = 30;
    myarr[3] = 40;
    myarr[4] = 50;
    for (int i = 0; i < 5; i++)
    {
        printf("myarr[%d] = %d\n", i, myarr[i]);
    }
}
```

Output:

```
myarr[0] = 10
myarr[1] = 20
myarr[2] = 30
myarr[3] = 40
myarr[4] = 50
```

In this example, the counter i represents an array element's index and the expression myarr[i] represents the array element's value.

9.3 Array Initialization

Instead of assigning array values one by one, we can also *initialize* the entire array using the *brace-enclosed list* {value1, value2, value3, ...}. Example:

```c
#include <stdio.h>

int main(void)
{
    int myarr[5] = {10, 20, 30, 40, 50};
    for (int i = 0; i < 5; i++)
    {
        printf("%d ", myarr[i]);
    }
}
```

Output:

---

10 20 30 40 50

This line – int myarr[5] = {10, 20, 30, 40, 50}; – declares and initializes an array of five elements using the values inside the initializer list { }.

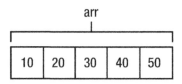

Figure 9-1. *An array of five integer numbers*

The comma-separated values (numbers in our case) inside the brace-init list { } are called *initializers*. The first array element is initialized with the first value inside the initializer list, which is 10. The second array element is initialized with the second value inside the list, which is 20, and so on.

Let us write an example that initializes the array and then uses the subscript operator to change the initial values of individual elements:

```c
#include <stdio.h>

int main(void)
```

```c
{
    int myarr[5] = {10, 20, 30, 40, 50}; /* initialize the array */
    for (int i = 0; i < 5; i++)
    {
        printf("%d ", myarr[i]);
    }
    printf("\n");
    myarr[0] = 100; /* change the value of the first element */
    myarr[2] = 300; /* change the value of the third element */
    for (int i = 0; i < 5; i++)
    {
        printf("%d ", myarr[i]);
    }
}
```

Output:

```
10 20 30 40 50
100 20 300 40 50
```

This example declares and initializes an array of five integers and prints out the entire array. Then, we assign new values to the first and the third array element using the subscript [ ] and the assignment operator = . As before, we print out the entire array using the for loop.

When using an initializer to define arrays, we do not have to specify the array length explicitly; the compiler will do this for us. Example:

```c
#include <stdio.h>

int main(void)
{
    int myarray[] = {10, 20, 30, 40, 50};
    for (int i = 0; i < 5; i++)
    {
        printf("%d ", myarray[i]);
    }
}
```

Output:

---

10 20 30 40 50

The compiler deduces the size of the array based on the number of initializers in the brace-enclosed list, which is 5. The array declaration would be identical to having `int myarray[5] = {10, 20, 30, 40, 50};`.

9.4 Character Arrays

To initialize an array of characters, we use the *string constant* as an initializer. Example:

```
#include <stdio.h>

int main(void)
{
    char myarray[] = "Hello";
    printf("%s", myarray);
}
```

Output:

Hello

The "Hello" is a *string constant,* also called a *character string literal.* It is an array of characters enclosed in double quotes (""). This string constant also has a hidden \0 character at the end, marking the end of a string:

H	e	l	l	o	\0

Figure 9-2. *A character array ending with a null terminating character*

Instead of using the `for` loop to print out the characters in an array, we used the `printf` function with the `%s` format specifier instead. The `%s` format specifier is used to print out the string characters.

The length of the "Hello" string constant is 6, five for the characters, plus one for the invisible *null terminator* \0 character. We did not specify the array size explicitly. But since we have the initializer, the compiler will deduce the size of the array to be 6 for us. It is the same as if we explicitly wrote char myarray[6] = "Hello";.

We use arrays when we want to group data objects of the same type. So instead of having to declare five individual variables of type int like int myvar1, myvar2, myvar3, myvar4, and myvar5;, we declare a single array variable having five elements: int myarr[5];.

9.5 Multidimensional Arrays

There are also arrays of arrays or the so-called *multidimensional arrays*. To declare a two-dimensional array, we use the following blueprint:

```
some_type myarr[number_of_rows][number_of_columns]
```

Let us write an example that declares and initializes an array of integers with two rows and three columns:

```
int main(void)
{
    int myarr[2][3] = {{1, 2, 3},
                       {4, 5, 6}};
}
```

This example defines a two-dimensional array with two rows (rows are horizontal) and three columns (columns are vertical). We used as many inner initialization lists as there are rows with as many elements as there are columns to initialize our entire array. The inner initialization lists {1, 2, 3} and {4, 5, 6} are comma-separated and surrounded by an outer initialization list.

To print out this two-dimensional array, we use two for loops. Example:

```
#include <stdio.h>

int main(void)
{
    int myarr[2][3] = {{1, 2, 3},
                       {4, 5, 6}};
```

```
    for (int i = 0; i < 2; i++)
    {
        for (int j = 0; j < 3; j++)
        {
            printf("%d ", myarr[i][j]);
        }
        printf("\n");
    }
}
```

Output:

```
1 2 3
4 5 6
```

The example initializes a two-dimensional array. We use two for loops to print out the values. There is one *outer* loop going from zero to 1, and there is one *inner* loop (the loop inside a loop) going from zero to 2. To access an element in a two-dimensional array, we use two subscript operators, one next to the other like myarr[row_index][column_index];. For example, to access the second element in a first row, we write myarr[0][1]; to access the third element in the first column, we write myarr[2][0]; and so on. The outer loop is used for indexing rows, and the inner loop is used for indexing columns. That way, we can loop through all the rows and all the columns and print out the array.

9.6 Array Size and Count

To determine the array size in bytes, we can use the sizeof operator. Example:

```
#include <stdio.h>

int main(void)
{
    int arr[3] = {1, 2, 3};
    size_t arrsize = sizeof(arr);
    printf("Total array size in bytes: %ld\n", arrsize);
}
```

Output:

```
Total array size in bytes: 12
```

This example uses the sizeof(arr) expression to determine the entire array's size in bytes. The size is equal to the size of int (which is probably 4 bytes on our machines) times the number of array elements, which is 3. So, depending on the machine and the compiler, the result will likely be equal to 12 bytes.

To obtain the number of elements in the array, we divide the total array size sizeof(arr) by the size of the type (sizeof(int) in our case). Example:

```c
#include <stdio.h>

int main(void)
{
    int arr[3] = {1, 2, 3};
    size_t arrcount = sizeof(arr) / sizeof(int);
    printf("The number of array elements is: %ld\n", arrcount);
}
```

Output:

```
The number of array elements is: 3
```

The number of elements can also be obtained by dividing the total array size by the size of the first array element sizeof(arr[0]):

```c
#include <stdio.h>

int main(void)
{
    int arr[3] = {1, 2, 3};
    size_t arrcount = sizeof(arr) / sizeof(arr[0]);
    printf("The number of array elements is: %ld\n", arrcount);
}
```

Output:

```
The number of array elements is: 3
```

Pointers

Data is stored in computer memory. The CPU reads from and writes to this memory. In simple terms, computer memory is an array of cells called bits. Usually, a group of eight bits makes a byte. Every byte in memory has its number, which we call *a (memory) address*. Our data objects reside in these memory cells, and each of these data objects has its address. If we know the address of an object, we can use pointers to access data objects in memory.

10.1 Introduction

So far, we have used regular variables to access these data objects in memory. Another way to manipulate data in these data objects is through pointers. A pointer is just like any other variable. It is of a certain type and has certain values. The type of the pointer is called a *pointer type*. The value of a pointer is the address of another variable/data object in memory. Since pointers hold addresses of other variables or array elements, we say they *point to* other objects.

10.2 Declaration and Initialization

To declare a pointer, we use the following syntax:

```
some_type* pointer_name;
```

The star symbol * after the type name signals this is a *pointer type*. To declare a pointer to int (a pointer to another variable of type int), we write int *p;, a pointer to type float is float *p;, a pointer to type char is char *p;, and so on.

Let us declare and initialize the pointer to int. To initialize the pointer with the address of another object, we use the address-of operator &. This operator returns the address (in memory) of its operand. Example:

© Slobodan Dmitrović 2024
S. Dmitrović, *Modern C for Absolute Beginners*, https://doi.org/10.1007/979-8-8688-0224-9_10

```
int main(void)
{
    int x = 123;
    int *p = &x;
}
```

Here, we declare a variable of type int and initialize it to a value of 123. Then, we declare a pointer of type int* and initialize it with the address of x. We say that p now *points to* x, and its value is the address of x in memory.

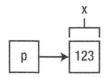

Figure 10-1. *A pointer pointing at an array*

To access the value the p points to, we prepend the pointer name with the * symbol as in *p. This * symbol is called the *dereference* operator. We say we *dereference the pointer.* This allows us to access and change the value pointed to by p:

```
#include <stdio.h>

int main(void)
{
    int x = 123;
    printf("The value before the change: %d\n", x);
    int* p = &x;
    *p = 456;
    printf("The value after the change: %d\n", x);
}
```

   Output:

```
The value before the change: 123
The value after the change: 456
```

We initialize a simple integer variable called x to the value of 123. Then, we declare a pointer and make it *point* to this variable (data object in memory) using the *address of* & operator. Then, we dereference the pointer with *p and assign a new value to the pointed-to object.

In a nutshell, *p *is* the value of x, and we use it to manipulate the value of x.

Let us now write an example where we have multiple pointers to multiple types:

```
#include <stdio.h>

int main(void)
{
    char c = 'a';
    int x = 123;
    float f = 456.789f;
    char *mycharp = &c;
    int *myintp = &x;
    float *myfloatp = &f;
    printf("The value of a pointed-to char: %c\n", *mycharp);
    printf("The value of a pointed-to int: %d\n", *myintp);
    printf("The value of a pointed-to float: %.3f\n", *myfloatp);
}
```

Output:

```
The value of a pointed-to char: a
The value of a pointed-to int: 123
The value of a pointed-to float: 456.789
```

Here, we define variables of type char, int, and float, respectively. Then, we declare pointers to each of these types and initialize them with the addresses of the variables. We print out the values of pointed-to objects by dereferencing the pointers.

There are a few points we should remember:

- We can declare a pointer type by placing a star next to the type name as in some_type* p; or placing a star symbol next to the variable name as in some_type *p;. It makes no difference. It is a matter of coding style and preference.

- When used in different contexts, the star symbol * means different things. When used in a declaration such as some_type *p;, it denotes a *pointer type*. When used in front of the variable name, as in the expressions *p; *or* *p = some_value;, the star symbol denotes a *dereferencing operator*.

We can reassign a pointer and make it point at another object in memory. Example:

```c
#include <stdio.h>

int main(void)
{
    int x = 10;
    int y = 20;
    printf("The value of x and y before the change: %d, %d\n", x, y);
    int *p;    /* declare a pointer to int called p */
    p = &x;    /* p points at x */
    *p = 100; /* change the value of x by dereferencing a pointer */
    p = &y;    /* p now points at y */
    *p = 200; /* change the value of y */
    printf("The value of x and y after the change: %d, %d\n", x, y);
}
```

Output:

```
The value of x and y before the change: 10, 20
The value of x and y after the change: 100, 200
```

Here, we define two integer variables. We then declare a pointer p and assign it the address of x with p = &x;. We then use the dereferenced pointer to access and change the value of x with *p = 100;. After that, we reassign a pointer to point at the y with p = &y. We then change the value of a pointed-to object (y) to 200 with *p = 200;. We print out the x and y values before and after the changes. Here, we used one pointer to change the values of several variables of the same type.

10.3 Pointers and Arrays

There are many similarities between arrays and pointers. We can use a pointer to point to an array and use it to access array elements. We simply assign the pointer to the array name. Example:

```
#include <stdio.h>

int main(void)
{
    int arr[5] = {10, 20, 30, 40, 50};
    int *p = arr; /* p now points at the first array element */
    printf("The first array element is: %d\n", *p);
}
```

   Output:

```
The first array element is: 10
```

The pointer now points at the first array element:

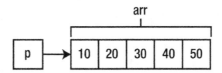

Figure 10-2. *A pointer pointing at the array's first element*

We can dereference a pointer using a subscript [] operator and use this technique to print out the entire array. Example:

```
#include <stdio.h>

int main(void)
{
    int arr[5] = {10, 20, 30, 40, 50};
    int *p = arr; /* p now points at the first array element */
    for (int i = 0; i < 5; i++)
```

```
        {
                printf("%d ", p[i]);
        }
}
```

Output:

---

10 20 30 40 50

The p[i] expression is equivalent to a *(p + i) expression. Each time, we increment the pointer value by i to point at the next array element. Then, we dereference the pointer and print the *pointed-to* value.

We can access individual array elements using a pointer. We simply use the address of an appropriate array element. If we want to access the first and the last array elements through a pointer, we write:

```
#include <stdio.h>

int main(void)
{
        int arr[5] = {10, 20, 30, 40, 50};
        for (int i = 0; i < 5; i++)
        {
                printf("%d ", arr[i]);
        }
        int *p;
        p = &arr[0]; /* get the address of the first array element */
        *p = 11;     /* change its value */
        p = &arr[4]; /* get the address of the last array element */
        *p = 55;     /* change its value */
        printf("\nAfter the changes:\n");
        for (int i = 0; i < 5; i++)
        {
                printf("%d ", arr[i]);
        }
}
```

Output:

```
10 20 30 40 50
After the changes:
11 20 30 40 55
```

This example defines an array of five integers and a pointer to int. We assign the address of the first array element to our pointer using the p = &arr[0]; statement. We change the element's value by dereferencing a pointer with *p = 11;. We repeat this process for the last array element arr[4]. Remember, array elements are indexed from 0, not 1. In an array declared as int arr[5];, the last array element is arr[4], not arr[5]. We assign the address of the last array element to our pointer with p = &arr[4];. By dereferencing a pointer, we change the pointed-to object's value with *p = 55;.

Note   When used as function arguments, arrays get converted to a pointer to the array's first element. We say the array *decays to a pointer*. If a function accepts a pointer type parameter, we can pass in either a *pointer variable* or an *array name variable* as an argument.

10.4 Pointer Arithmetics

The expressions &arr[0] and arr are equivalent, as the name of the array arr is also an address of the first element in an array. The previous example will serve as an introduction to *pointer arithmetic*. We can apply arithmetic operators to pointers and add or subtract numbers to and from a pointer. For example, let us have a pointer that points at the first array element, similar to what we had in the previous example:

```
#include <stdio.h>

int main(void)
{
    int arr[5] = {10, 20, 30, 40, 50};
    int* p = arr; /* the same as int *p = &arr[0]; */
    printf("The pointed-to value is: %d.\n", *p);
```

```
        p++;
        printf("The pointed-to value is: %d.\n", *p);
}
```

Output:

```
The pointed-to value is: 10.
The pointed-to value is: 20.
```

This example defines an array of five integers and initializes the pointer to point to the first array element with int *p = arr;. We print out the value by dereferencing a pointer with *p. We then increment the pointer by one by applying the ++ operator. What does it mean to increment the pointer by one? It means that it now points at the next data object in memory. And since array elements are positioned sequentially in memory, the pointer now points to the next array element, which has a value of 20. The pointer is incremented by *one times the size of the type of the element* it points to. The number we add to the pointer scales to the size of the pointed-to object; it scales to the number of bytes of that object.

If we wanted to print out the third array element, we would add 2 to the pointer:

```
#include <stdio.h>

int main(void)
{
        int arr[5] = {10, 20, 30, 40, 50};
        int* p = arr; /* the same as int* p = &arr[0]; */
        p += 2;
        printf("The pointed-to value is: %d.\n", *p);
}
```

Output:

```
The pointed-to value is: 30.
```

Here, we define an array of five elements and make our pointer point to the first element in an array.

Then we increment the pointer by 2 so that it now *moves by two integer places in memory and points* at the third array element. When adding 2 to our pointer, the actual value of the pointer is incremented by *2 times the size of an* int. But for us, it just increments by two (integers).

Note   Adding/subtracting/multiplying pointers of different types is **not** allowed.

10.5 Void Pointers

Pointers point only to specific types. A pointer of type int* can only point to an int value in memory. It cannot point to, for example, a float. But the pointer of type void* can point to *any type*. All pointer types are implicitly convertible to type void*. The void* type is also called a *pointer to void* or a *generic pointer type*. Let us write a simple example that uses a void* pointer to access the value of an int* pointer:

```
#include <stdio.h>

int main(void)
{
        int x = 123;
        int *ip = &x; // get an address of an integer object
        void *vp;
        vp = ip; // void pointer gets the value of an integer pointer
        printf("The pointed-to value is: %d\n", *((int *)vp));
}
```

Output:

```
The pointed-to value is: 123
```

This example defines a pointer of type int* and then assigns that value to a void pointer. Void pointers must be cast to the appropriate pointer type before they are dereferenced. So, we are not allowed to type the *vp;. First, we must cast the void pointer to the appropriate pointer type. In our case, it is the int* type, and we use the (int*)vp expression. Only then can we dereference the entire expression with *(int*(vp));.

One use of the void* type is when printing out the value of a pointer (the memory address it points to). To print out the value of a pointer, we need to cast/convert the pointer to type void* using the (void*)some_pointer_name syntax and then utilize the %p format specifier. Example:

```
#include <stdio.h>

int main(void)
{
    char c = 'a';
    int x = 123;
    float f = 456.789f;
    char *mycharp = &c;
    int *myintp = &x;
    float *myfloatp = &f;
    printf("The value of a char pointer: %p\n", (void *)mycharp);
    printf("The value of an int pointer: %p\n", (void *)myintp);
    printf("The value of a float pointer: %p\n", (void *)myfloatp);
}
```

Output:

```
The value of a char pointer: 0x7ffd3dbcde17
The value of an int pointer: 0x7ffd3dbcde18
The value of a float pointer: 0x7ffd3dbcde1c
```

The value printed out using the %p specifier is the value of the pointer itself. That value is the memory address of another object. Depending on the C implementation, this address value might be printed out as a hexadecimal number similar to 0x7ffd3dbcde1c.

Note   This example prints the value of the pointer itself, not the value of the pointed-to object. The value of a pointed-to object is obtained by dereferencing a pointer.

All pointers can also have a special value of NULL. When a pointer has a value of NULL, it *does not point to any other object.* We say it *points to nothing* or it is a *NULL pointer.* The value of NULL can be used to initialize pointers to point to nothing. Example:

```c
#include <stdio.h>

int main(void)
{
    char* mycharp = NULL;
    int* myintp = NULL;
    float* myfloatp = NULL;
    printf("The value of a char pointer: %p\n", (void *)mycharp);
    printf("The value of an int pointer: %p\n", (void *)myintp);
    printf("The value of a float pointer: %p\n", (void *)myfloatp);
}
```

Output:

```
The value of a char pointer: (nil)
The value of an int pointer: (nil)
The value of a float pointer: (nil)
```

Note   Pointer arithmetics on a **void** pointer is **not** allowed.

10.6 Pointer to Character Arrays

We can initialize a pointer with a string constant such as "Hello World!".

```c
#include <stdio.h>

int main(void)
{
    char* p = "Hello World!";
    printf("%s", p);
}
```

Output:

```
Hello World!
```

The string constant "Hello World!" is an array of characters enclosed in double quotes. Our char* pointer p points at the beginning of that array – at the first element. We use the %s format specifier to print out the entire string pointed by p. The %s specifier prints out the entire string pointed to by p. The %c format specifier prints out only one (the first) character in a string when using a dereferenced string pointer *p. Example:

```
#include <stdio.h>

int main(void)
{
    char* p = "Hello World!";
    printf("%c", *p);
}
```

Output:

```
H
```

10.7 Arrays of Pointers

Since a pointer type is just another type, we can have *arrays of pointers*. To declare an array of pointers, we use the following syntax:

```
some_type* pointer_name[number_of_elements];
```

One use case is an array of char* type. To declare an array of pointers to char, we write:

```
#include <stdio.h>

int main(void)
{
    char *p[] = {"First sentence.",
                 "Second sentence.",
                 "Third sentence."};
```

```
    for (int i = 0; i < 3; i++)
    {
            printf("%s\n", p[i]);
    }
}
```

Output:

```
First sentence.
Second sentence.
Third sentence.
```

This statement:

```
char *p[] = {"First sentence", "Second sentence.", "Third sentence."};
```

declares an array of three pointers of type char* and initializes them with string constants. The compiler inserts the number 3 as a length of our array, and the statement now becomes char *p[3];. These three pointers point at three different character strings. We can look at these strings as having three separate sentences.

We then use the for loop to print out all three sentences by accessing an appropriate pointer through a subscript operator as in p[i]. So p[0] points at the "First sentence.", p[1] points at the "Second sentence.", and p[2] points at the "Third sentence.".

The subscript operator [] acts as a dereference operator as the p[i] expression is equivalent to *(p+i). Using a subscript operator with an index on a pointer as in p[i] means *incrementing a pointer by* i *places and dereferencing it.*

Note   So far, we have used pointers with automatic variables. In later chapters, we will explore how pointers are used in dynamic memory allocations.

CHAPTER 11

Command-Line Arguments

There is another `main` function signature that allows us to work with the command-line arguments. These are arguments we can pass to our executable file in the command line. Example:

```
myexe param1 param2
```

Here, the `myexe` is the name of our executable file, and `param1` and `param2` are some arbitrary arguments we pass in. The function `main` that allows us to parse these arguments has the following signature:

```
int main(int argc, char *argv[])
```

The `argc` is the number of command-line arguments we pass to our executable. The `argv` is the pointer to an array of strings that represent the arguments. If we pass no arguments to our executable file, the `argc` is 1. The first element in an array of strings, `argv[0]`, is the name of our executable file. Suppose we pass two parameters to our executable file, as in the preceding example. In that case, the `argc` is equal to 3 as there are three arguments in total, one that represents the name of our executable and the additional two arguments, `param1` and `param2`, we explicitly pass in. In that case, `argv[1]` is equal to `param1`, and `argv[2]` is equal to `param2`. Example:

```
#include <stdio.h>

int main(int argc, char *argv[])
{
    printf("The command-line arguments are:\n");
    for (int i = 0; i < argc; i++)
```

© Slobodan Dmitrović 2024
S. Dmitrović, *Modern C for Absolute Beginners*, https://doi.org/10.1007/979-8-8688-0224-9_11

```
    {
            printf("%s\n", argv[i]);
    }
}
```

If we invoke our executable with `./a.out param1 param2`, the output would be:

```
The command-line arguments are:
./a.out
param1
param2
```

CHAPTER 12

Exercises

12.1 Character Array

Write a program that defines and initializes a character array. Print the array using the %s format specifier:

```c
#include <stdio.h>

int main(void)
{
    char arr[] = "Hello World!";
    printf("The value is: %s\n", arr);
}
```

Output:

```
The value is: Hello World!
```

12.2 Array Elements

Write a program that defines and initializes an array of five integers. Change the values of the first and last array elements. Print out the array:

```c
#include <stdio.h>

int main(void)
{
    int arr[] = {10, 20, 30, 40, 50};
    arr[0] = 11; // change the first element
```

© Slobodan Dmitrović 2024
S. Dmitrović, *Modern C for Absolute Beginners*, https://doi.org/10.1007/979-8-8688-0224-9_12

```
        arr[4] = 55; // change the last element
        for (int i = 0; i < 5; i++)
        {
            printf("%d ", arr[i]);
        }
}
```

Output:

```
11 20 30 40 55
```

12.3 Pointer to an Existing Object

Write a program that defines a simple double variable and a pointer that points to that variable. Print the variable's value by dereferencing a pointer. Then, change the variable's value by dereferencing a pointer:

```
#include <stdio.h>

int main(void)
{
    double d = 123.456;
    double *p = &d;
    printf("The value before the change is: %f\n", *p);
    *p = 789.101;
    printf("The value after the change is: %f\n", *p);
}
```

Output:

```
The value before the change is: 123.456000
The value after the change is: 789.101000
```

12.4 Pointers and Arrays

Write a program that defines an array of five integers. Use a pointer to print out the entire array:

```
#include <stdio.h>

int main(void)
{
        int arr[] = {10, 20, 30, 40, 50};
        int *p = arr;
        for (int i = 0; i < 5; i++)
        {
                printf("%d\n", p[i]);
        }
}
```

   Output:

```
10 20 30 40 50
```

12.5 Pointer to a Character Array

Write a program that defines a pointer to a character array. Print the character array using a pointer:

```
#include <stdio.h>

int main(void)
{
        char *p = "This is a character array.";
        printf("The result is: %s", p);
}
```

   Output:

```
The result is: This is a character array.
```

12.6 Pointer Arithmetics

Write a program that defines an array of five integers. Use pointer arithmetics to print out the third and fourth array elements:

```c
#include <stdio.h>

int main(void)
{
    int arr[] = {10, 20, 30, 40, 50};
    int *p = arr;
    p += 2; // p now points at the third array element
    printf("The third array element is: %d\n", *p);
    p += 1; // p now points at the fourth array element
    printf("The fourth array element is: %d\n", *p);
}
```

Output:

```
The third array element is: 30
The fourth array element is: 40
```

12.7 Array of Pointers

Write a program that defines an array of four pointers to sentences. Sentences themselves are arrays of characters:

```c
#include <stdio.h>

int main(void)
{
    char *p[] = {"This is the first sentence.",
                 "This is the second sentence.",
                 "This is the third sentence.",
                 "This is the last sentence."};
    for (int i = 0; i < 4; i++)
    {
```

```
        printf("%s\n", p[i]);
    }
}
```

Output:

```
This is the first sentence.
This is the second sentence.
This is the third sentence.
This is the last sentence.
```

CHAPTER 13

Functions

In short, functions are named reusable pieces of code. A function is made up of a function body associated with a function name. A function can accept zero or more parameters and optionally return a result.

13.1 Introduction

A function has a type, a name, a list of optional parameters, and a function body. The function blueprint is of the following syntax:

```
some_type function_name(optional_parameters_declarations)
{
    // function body with declarations and statements
    return some_value; // optional return statement
}
```

So far, we have used only a main() function, which is the main program entry point. Let us now learn how to create our *user-defined functions*. The following program defines a simple user-defined function that outputs a "Hello World from a function." message and calls(invokes) this function from our main program. Example:

```
#include <stdio.h>

void printMessage(void)
{
    printf("Hello World from a function.\n");
}

int main(void)
{
    printMessage();
}
```

© Slobodan Dmitrović 2024
S. Dmitrović, *Modern C for Absolute Beginners*, https://doi.org/10.1007/979-8-8688-0224-9_13

Output:

```
Hello World from a function.
```

Here, we define a function called printMessage() before our main() function. The printMessage(void) function outputs a simple message to the console window. The function is of type void, followed by a function name printMessage followed by an empty list of parameters inside parentheses indicated by (void) followed by a function body marked with braces {}. Inside a function body, we execute statements. In our case, it is a simple printf statement that outputs a message.

We call the printmessage function from our main program by specifying a function name followed by parentheses printMessage();. We also say we *invoke the function*.

Let us now write a function called mySum() that sums the two integer numbers and returns a result:

```c
#include <stdio.h>

int mySum(int x, int y)
{
    return x + y;
}

int main(void)
{
    int myresult = mySum(10, 20);
    printf("The result is: %d\n", myresult);
}
```

Output:

```
The result is: 30
```

This example defines a function called mySum. The function is of type int and accepts two parameters we named x and y. Both parameters are of type int. We declare these two parameters by specifying their types and names. We separate the declarations with a comma sign as with int x, int y function parameters signature.

The `return` statement terminates the function and returns the result of the x + y expression to the *function call expression,* which in our case is the mySum(10, 20) expression. We sometimes simplify and say the `return` statement assigns the value of the x + y expression to our mySum function.

We then call/invoke the mySum function in our main program by writing the function name followed by the actual *arguments* for our parameters inside parentheses as in mySum(10, 20);. The first parameter, x, now becomes (receives a value of) 10, and the second parameter, y, now becomes 20. The function performs the calculation, and the `return` statement assigns the value of an x + y expression to a function call expression mySum(10, 20) and *returns the control* to our caller. A *caller* is another function that calls/invokes our function. In this case, our main() function is the *caller* as it *calls* the mySum() function. The main program assigns the value of the mySum() function to a local variable mySum and prints out the result.

13.2 Function Declaration

We can split (organize, divide) the function into a function declaration and a function definition. A function declaration *introduces* the function type, name, and parameter declarations list into the current scope. A function declaration does not have a function body and ends with a semicolon. The blueprint for the function declaration is:

```
some_type function_name(optional_parameters_declarations);
```

Let us write an example that declares a simple function called myFunction that accepts no parameters and does not return a value:

```
#include <stdio.h>

void myFunction(void);

int main(void)
{
    printf("Function declared.");
}
```

Output:

```
Function declared.
```

The function's return type void indicates the function does not return a value. The void inside parentheses (void) indicates the function accepts no parameters.

To declare a function that accepts two integer parameters and returns an integer type, we write:

```
#include <stdio.h>

int myFunction(int x, int y);

int main(void)
{
    printf("Function declared.\n");
}
```

Output:

```
Function declared.
```

When declaring a function that has parameters, we can omit the names of the parameters and supply only the parameter types:

```
#include <stdio.h>

int myFunction(int, int);

int main(void)
{
    printf("Function declared.\n");
}
```

Output:

```
Function declared.
```

If you are asking yourself "What is the point of these function declarations?" you are asking a valid question. The answer is as follows:

The function can indeed be split into a function declaration and a function definition. If we declare a function, we assume it is defined somewhere else. By declaring a function, we are saying to our compiler/linker: "There is this function called *myFunction*, and I know for sure it is fully defined somewhere else, whether in an external source file or a library. So here is the function declaration, and I want to be able to call this function from my program." The compiler and linker then search for the function definition by following a set of predetermined rules. We discuss these in more detail later in the book.

In general, we keep the function declarations in header files (.h files), and we keep the function definitions in source files (.c files). This way, we separate the declarations from the implementations (definitions). Indeed, if we open a header file that is part of the standard library, we will see a lot of function declarations there. In our examples earlier, we put the function declarations in .c files for illustrative purposes.

For example, the printf function is declared inside the <stdio.h> header file. And when we want to use the printf function in our main program, we must include this header file.

13.3 Function Definition

A function definition is a whole function with a function signature plus the function body. To define a function, we use the following blueprint:

```
some_type function_name(optional_parameters_declarations)
{
    // function body with declarations and statements
    return some_value; // optional return statement
}
```

To define a simple function that outputs a simple message and accepts no parameters, we write:

```
#include <stdio.h>

void myFunction(void)
{
    printf("Function defined.\n");
}
```

```
int main(void)
{
    myFunction();
}
```

Output:

```
Function defined.
```

To define a function of type int that returns the sum of two integer parameters, we write:

```
#include <stdio.h>

int myFunction(int x, int y)
{
    return x + y;
}

int main(void)
{
    int myresult = myFunction(10, 20);
    printf("The result is: %d\n", myresult);
}
```

Output:

```
The result is: 30
```

While the function declaration can be placed inside another function's body, a function definition must be placed outside any other function's body, including the function main. We say we place the function definition in a *file scope*.

Notice how we placed the myFunction definition before the main's definition. If we place the user-defined function definition after the main's definition, there will be a compiler error. The compiler encounters a function call myFunction(10, 20); inside a main's body but does not know what function this is. To overcome this, we can put a function declaration before the main's body and the function definition after the main's body. The program now compiles successfully:

```
#include <stdio.h>

//function declaration
int myFunction(int x, int y);
int main(void)
{
     int myresult = myFunction(10, 20);
     printf("The result is: %d\n", myresult);
}

// function definition
int myFunction(int x, int y)
{
     return x + y;
}
```

Output:

The result is: 30

13.4 Parameters and Arguments

Parameters are variable declarations inside parentheses in a function declaration or a function definition. A function can have zero, one, or a fixed number of parameters. If a function accepts no parameters, we write my_function_name(void). If it has one parameter, we use the following blueprint: my_function_name(some_type parameter_name). If a function has a fixed number of parameters, we use the comma-separated declarations like my_function_name(some_type param_name1, some_type param_name2).

Let us write an example that demonstrates the use of no parameters function:

```
#include <stdio.h>

void myFunction(void)
{
     printf("No parameters function.\n");
}
```

```
int main(void)
{
    myFunction();
}
```

Output:

```
No parameters function.
```

When we define a function that accepts no parameters, we use the (void) function signature. When calling a function, we simply use the function call operator () as in myFunction();.

An example that uses a function accepting one parameter:

```
#include <stdio.h>

int myFunction(int x)
{
    return x;
}

int main(void)
{
    int myresult;
    myresult = myFunction(5);
    printf("One parameter function result: %d\n", myresult);
}
```

Output:

```
One parameter function result: 5
```

We defined a function that accepts one parameter. The x parameter in the function definition is also called a *formal parameter*. We then call the function in our main program and pass it a value of 5. This value is called an *argument*. So, argument 5 replaces the formal parameter x. Wherever there was a formal parameter x in our function, we now use the actual value of 5 to do whatever calculation is needed.

We can also use local variables as arguments. Example:

```c
#include <stdio.h>

int myFunction(int x)
{
    return x;
}

int main(void)
{
    int myint = 5;
    int myresult;
    myresult = myFunction(myint);
    printf("One parameter function result: %d\n", myresult);
}
```

Output:

```
One parameter function result: 5
```

Here we used the local variable myint as a function argument. So now x gets the value of myint, which is 5. More precisely, it gets a copy of the value of myint, as arguments are passed *by value*. The function makes a copy of myint and works on that copy. Any changes done to a parameter inside a function do not affect the original myint variable.

To use a function with multiple parameters, we can write:

```c
#include <stdio.h>

int myFunction(int x, int y)
{
    return x + y;
}

int main(void)
{
```

```
        int myresult;
        myresult = myFunction(10, 20);
        printf("Two parameters function result: %d\n", myresult);
}
```

Output:

```
Two parameters function result: 30
```

In this example, we defined a function accepting two parameters. We separate the parameter declarations with a comma, as in (int x, int y). We then call a function and supply two comma-separated arguments, 10 and 20, as in myfunction(10, 20). Parameter x now takes the value of 10, and parameter y receives the value of 20.

As before, we can use the local variables as arguments:

```
#include <stdio.h>

int myFunction(int x, int y)
{
        return x + y;
}

int main(void)
{
        int a = 10;
        int b = 20;
        int myresult;
        myresult = myFunction(a, b);
        printf("Two parameters function result: %d\n", myresult);
}
```

Output:

```
Two parameters function result: 30
```

13.4.1 Passing Arguments

Arguments, in general, can be passed *by value* or by *reference/pointer/address*. By default, all arguments are passed *by value* in C. Here, we discuss both scenarios.

Passing by Value

When we pass an argument to a function, a function makes an internal copy of that argument's value and works on that copy. The original argument value is unaffected. For example, let us have a function that has one parameter and assigns a new value to that parameter inside the function body:

```c
#include <stdio.h>

void myFunction(int x)
{
    x = 456;
}

int main(void)
{
    int a = 123;
    printf("The value before the function call: %d\n", a);
    myFunction(a);
    printf("The value after the function call: %d\n", a);
}
```

Output:

```
The value before the function call: 123
The value after the function call: 123
```

The function has a parameter x that takes the value of the argument a. The function makes a copy of a and does not affect the original a variable. The value of a remains the same before and after the function call. The function makes temporary copies of a and works on those copies, not the argument a itself.

Passing by Pointer/Address

To change the actual values of arguments a using a function, we use the pointer type parameter in the function signature. And when we call the function, we supply the address of the argument using an *address-of operator* &. Let us rewrite the preceding example so that the function changes the value of argument a:

```c
#include <stdio.h>

void myFunction(int *x)
{
    *x = 456;
}
int main(void)
{
    int a = 123;
    printf("The value before the function call: %d\n", a);
    myFunction(&a);
    printf("The value after the function call: %d\n", a);
}
```

Output:

```
The value before the function call: 123
The value after the function call: 456
```

The function accepts a pointer to int. It then dereferences the pointer and assigns a new value to a pointed-to object. We then call the function, and instead of supplying a as an argument name, we supply the addresses of a by using &a. The function is now able to modify the argument itself. This trick allows us to mimic the behavior of *passing by reference* present in other languages.

Note   By default, all arguments are passed by copy/value, and the function cannot modify the arguments' values. Using pointer parameters and addresses of arguments, we can pass arguments by address/reference and change the arguments' values.

13.5 Return Statement

The return statement inside our function body is of the following syntax:

```
return;
return some_expression_or_value;
```

The return statements *return* a control (of the program flow) and a value to the caller/calling function. But in everyday life, we simply say it *returns a value to our function*. However, the correct way to put it is to say it *returns a value to our function call*, the place where our function is called using the myFunction(); statement. An example with a simple function that returns a hard-coded integer value of 10:

```
#include <stdio.h>
int myFunction()
{
      return 10;
}
int main(void)
{
      int x;
      x = myFunction();
      printf("The function returned a value of: %d\n", x);
}
```

Output:

```
The function returned a value of: 10
```

The return statement causes our function to exit. Statements following the return statement will not be executed. Example:

```
#include <stdio.h>
int myFunction()
{
      return 10;
      printf("This statement will not be executed.\n");
}
```

```c
int main(void)
{
    int x;
    x = myFunction();
    printf("The function returned a value of: %d\n", x);
}
```

Output:

```
The function returned a value of: 10
```

A function can have multiple return statements. Example:

```c
#include <stdio.h>

int myFunction(int a)
{
    if (a > 0)
    {
        return 1;
    }
    if (a < 0)
    {
        return -1;
    }
    return 0;
}

int main(void)
{
    int x;
    x = myFunction(10);
    printf("The function returned a value of: %d\n", x);
}
```

Output:

```
The function returned a value of: 1
```

This function has three `return` statements, but only one of them will be executed. When any of these is encountered, the function will return the value and the control to the caller. The remaining statements in the function body will not be executed. Return values of 1, 0, and -1 are here for illustrative purposes.

CHAPTER 14

Exercises

14.1 A Simple Function

Write a program that defines a function of type void called printMessage(). The function outputs a simple message on the standard output. Call the user-defined function from the main function:

```
#include <stdio.h>

void printMessage()
{
      printf("Hello World! from a function.\n");
}

int main(void)
{
      printMessage();
}
```

Output:

```
Hello World! from a function.
```

14.2 Function Declaration and Definition

Write a program that declares and defines a function of type void called printMessage(). The function outputs a simple message on the standard output. Call the user-defined function from the main function:

© Slobodan Dmitrović 2024
S. Dmitrović, *Modern C for Absolute Beginners*, https://doi.org/10.1007/979-8-8688-0224-9_14

```
#include <stdio.h>

void printMessage(); // function declaration

int main(void)
{
    printMessage(); // function call
}

void printMessage() // function definition
{
    printf("Hello World! from a function.\n");
}
```

Output:

```
Hello World! from a function.
```

14.3 Passing Arguments by Value

Write a program that defines a function that accepts a single argument by value. In its body, the function increments an argument by one. Invoke the function in the main program:

```
#include <stdio.h>

void byValue(int arg)
{
    arg++;
}

int main(void)
{
    int x = 123;
    printf("The value before the function call: %d\n", x);
    byValue(x);
    printf("The value after the function call: %d\n", x);
}
```

Output:

```
The value before the function call: 123
The value after the function call: 123
```

14.4 Passing Arguments by Pointer/Address

Write a program that defines a function that accepts a single argument by a pointer (an address). In its body, the function increments an argument by one. Invoke the function in the main program by passing in the address of a local variable:

```c
#include <stdio.h>

void byAddress(int *arg)
{
        (*arg)++;
}

int main(void)
{
        int x = 123;
        printf("The value before the function call: %d\n", x);
        byAddress(&x);
        printf("The value after the function call: %d\n", x);
}
```

Output:

```
The value before the function call: 123
The value after the function call: 124
```

14.5 Function – Multiple Parameters

Write a program that defines a function called multiply. The function accepts two arguments of type int, multiplies them, and returns a result. Invoke the function inside the function main. Assign the result of a function call to a local variable and print the result:

```
#include <stdio.h>

int multiply(int a, int b)
{
    return a * b;
}

int main(void)
{
    int x = 123;
    int y = 456;
    int z = multiply(x, y);
    printf("The result is: %d\n", z);
}
```

   Output:

```
The result is: 56088
```

CHAPTER 15

Structures

A structure is a type that has *members*. These members can be variables of other types.

15.1 Introduction

The structure declaration is of the following syntax:

```
struct some_name
{
    type_name member_name_1;
    type_name member_name_2;
    // ...
};
```

A structure is also a *type*. The name of this type is the name of the structure. A structure is a collection of variables, an excellent way to group the variables and organize data.

Let us write a simple example that declares a structure with three members:

```
#include <stdio.h>

struct MyStruct
{
    char c;
    int x;
    double d;
};
```

© Slobodan Dmitrović 2024
S. Dmitrović, *Modern C for Absolute Beginners*, https://doi.org/10.1007/979-8-8688-0224-9_15

```
int main(void)
{
    printf("Declared a structure of type: struct MyStruct.\n");
}
```

Output:

```
Declared a structure of type: struct MyStruct.
```

This example declares a structure called MyStruct. The structure name MyStruct is also called a *tag*. This structure has three different members. The first member is of type char and is called c. The remaining two members are of other types, and we gave them different names, x and d. The structure declaration ends with a semicolon after the closing brace as in };.

We can now declare a variable s of this struct MyStruct type either by placing the variable name after the structure's closing brace:

```
#include <stdio.h>

struct MyStruct
{
    char c;
    int x;
    double d;
} s;

int main(void)
{
    printf("Structure type struct MyStruct declared.\n");
    printf("Variable s of type struct MyStruct declared.\n");
}
```

Output:

```
Structure type struct MyStruct declared.
Variable s of type struct MyStruct declared.
```

---

or by writing struct MyStruct s; inside the main function:

```c
#include <stdio.h>

struct MyStruct
{
    char c;
    int x;
    double d;
};

int main(void)
{
    printf("Structure type struct MyStruct declared.\n");
    struct MyStruct s;
    printf("Variable s of type struct MyStruct declared.\n");
}
```

Both examples declare a structure called MyStruct and a variable s of that struct MyStruct type. We say that s is a structure of type struct MyStruct type. We can eliminate the lengthy struct MyStruct wording when defining a structure type by utilizing the typedef declaration:

```c
#include <stdio.h>

typedef struct MyStruct MyStruct;

struct MyStruct
{
    char c;
    int x;
    double d;
};

int main(void)
{
    MyStruct s;
    printf("Variable s of type MyStruct declared.\n");
}
```

The `typedef struct MyStruct MyStruct;` statement creates an *alias* for a `struct MyStruct` type. This alias is now simply called `MyStruct`, so we can now omit the `struct` part when declaring a variable of this type.

Another way to create an alias for a structure type is to use the following code:

```c
#include <stdio.h>

typedef struct
{
    char c;
    int x;
    double d;
} MyStruct;

int main(void)
{
    MyStruct s;
    printf("Variable s of type MyStruct declared.\n");
}
```

15.2 Initialization

A structure can be *initialized* by providing an initializer list with comma-separated values, as in {value_1, value_2, value_n}:

```c
#include <stdio.h>

typedef struct
{
    char c;
    int x;
    double d;
} MyStruct;

int main(void)
{
    MyStruct s = {'a', 123, 456.789};
    printf("Variable s of type MyStruct initialized.\n");
```

```
    printf("Member c has a value of %c\n", s.c);
    printf("Member x has a value of %d\n", s.x);
    printf("Member d has a value of %f\n", s.d);
}
```

Output:

```
Variable s of type MyStruct initialized.
Member c has a value of a
Member x has a value of 123
Member d has a value of 456.789000
```

Member c is initialized with a value of 'a', member x is initialized with a value of 123, and member d receives a value of 456.789. Members are initialized in the order in which they are declared.

We can also initialize a structure using the so-called *designated initializers*. These allow us to initialize the structure not just in the order in which the members are declared but in *any order*. We specify the member name and the value for that particular member using the {.member_name_1 = value_1, .member_name_2 = value_2, .member_name_n = value_n} syntax. Example:

```
#include <stdio.h>
typedef struct
{
    char c;
    int x;
    double d;
} MyStruct;
int main(void)
{
    MyStruct s = {.x = 123, .c = 'a', .d = 456.789};
    printf("Variable s of type MyStruct initialized.\n");
    printf("Member c has a value of %c\n", s.c);
    printf("Member x has a value of %d\n", s.x);
    printf("Member d has a value of %f\n", s.d);
}
```

Here, we initialized member x first, then c, and then d. We print out the values of individual members using the *member access operator* (.).

The following variant, where we declare a structure and initialize a variable in the same statement, is also valid:

```
#include <stdio.h>

struct MyStruct
{
    char c;
    int x;
    double d;
} s = {'c', 123, 456.789};

int main(void)
{
    printf("Structure initialized.\n");
    printf("Member c has a value of %c\n", s.c);
    printf("Member x has a value of %d\n", s.x);
    printf("Member d has a value of %f\n", s.d);
}
```

15.3 Member Access Operator

To access individual structure members, we use the variable s name, followed by a *member access operator* ., followed by the name of the appropriate member:

```
#include <stdio.h>

typedef struct
{
    char c;
    int x;
    double d;
} MyStruct;

int main(void)
{
```

```
    MyStruct s = {'a', 123, 456.789};
    printf("Variable s of type MyStruct initialized.\n");
    printf("Member c has a value of %c\n", s.c);
    printf("Member x has a value of %d\n", s.x);
    printf("Member d has a value of %f\n", s.d);
}
```

Output:

```
Variable s of type MyStruct initialized.
Member c has a value of a
Member x has a value of 123
Member d has a value of 456.789000
```

Here, we access and print out the individual members by using the variable_name. member_name syntax as in s.c, s.x, and s.d. This *member access operator* . is also referred to as a *dot operator.*

To access and change the values of individual members, we write:

```
#include <stdio.h>

typedef struct
{
    char c;
    int x;
    double d;
} MyStruct;

int main(void)
{
    MyStruct s = {'a', 123, 456.789};
    printf("Variable s of type MyStruct initialized.\n");
    printf("Changing member values...\n");
    s.c = 'b';
    s.x = 456;
    s.d = 789.101;
    printf("Member c has a value of %c\n", s.c);
```

```
    printf("Member x has a value of %d\n", s.x);
    printf("Member d has a value of %f\n", s.d);
}
```

Output:

```
Variable s of type MyStruct initialized.
Changing member values...
Member c has a value of b
Member x has a value of 456
Member d has a value of 789.101000
```

In this example, we used the member access operator to access, change, and print out the values of individual members.

15.4 Copying Structures

We can assign (copy) one variable of type struct to another variable of the same type. When assigning, we are copying member values, the assignment operator = copies member values:

```
#include <stdio.h>

typedef struct
{
    char c;
    int x;
    double d;
} MyStruct;

int main(void)
{
    MyStruct s1 = {'a', 123, 456.789};
    MyStruct s2;
    s2 = s1; /* copies member values */
    printf("Values from s1 copied to s2.\n");
    printf("Member s2.c has a value of %c\n", s2.c);
```

```
    printf("Member s2.x has a value of %d\n", s2.x);
     printf("Member s2.d has a value of %f\n", s2.d);
}
```

Output:

```
Values from s1 copied to s2.
Member s2.c has a value of a
Member s2.x has a value of 123
Member s2.d has a value of 456.789000
```

In this example, we have two variables of the MyStruct type, named s1 and s2. We initialized s1 with some arbitrary values. Then we copied values from s1 to s2 using the s2 = s1; statement. We can also say we *assigned* s1 to s2. The copy of the s1's member values is made and then assigned to appropriate s2 members. Now, both struct variables have identical values. Remember, at this point, changing the value of one structure does not affect the value of another and vice versa.

15.5 Pointers to Structures

We can also use *pointers to structures*. Let us see how to create a pointer to a structure and assign it an address of an existing structure variable:

```
#include <stdio.h>

struct MyStruct
{
    char c;
    int x;
    double d;
};

int main(void)
{
    struct MyStruct s = {'a', 123, 456.789};
    struct MyStruct *ps = &s;
    printf("Member c has a value of %c\n", (*ps).c);
```

```
    printf("Member x has a value of %d\n", (*ps).x);
    printf("Member d has a value of %f\n", (*ps).d);
}
```

Output:

```
Member c has a value of a
Member x has a value of 123
Member d has a value of 456.789000
```

Here, we declared a simple structure. Then, in the main program, we initialized a variable s of that struct MyStruct type. Then, we declared a variable ps, which is a pointer to that structure type. We initialize this variable with the address of a data object s. To access a structure member via a pointer, we dereference the pointer using a * symbol. We then use the member access operator, followed by a member name as in (*ps).c, to access and print the member value. The . operator has higher precedence than the * operator, so we must use parentheses to ensure the dereferencing happens before the member access.

Another way to access the structure member through a pointer is by using the *arrow operator* ->. This operator both dereferences the pointer to a structure and accesses a member. Example:

```
#include <stdio.h>

typedef struct
{
    char c;
    int x;
    double d;
} MyStruct;

int main(void)
{
    MyStruct s = {'a', 123, 456.789};
    MyStruct *ps = &s;
    printf("Member c has a value of %c\n", ps->c);
```

```
    printf("Member x has a value of %d\n", ps->x);
    printf("Member d has a value of %f\n", ps->d);
}
```

Output:

```
Member c has a value of a
Member x has a value of 123
Member d has a value of 456.789000
```

The use of an -> operator replaces the need for both the dereference (*) and member access operator (.), as it does both operations. To access a single member, instead of having to write the (*ps).c expression, we simply write ps->c.

15.6 Self-Referencing Structures

A structure can have a field that is a pointer to the structure type itself. This field is not an instance of a structure but a pointer to a structure type. Example:

```
struct MyStruct
{
    int x;
    struct MyStruct* next;
};
```

This declaration allows us to create multiple objects of type struct MyStruct representing a *singly linked list*.

To declare a structure that can represent a *doubly linked list*, we need two pointer fields, one that will point to the previous element in the list and another that will point to the next element in the list. Example:

```
struct MyStruct
{
    int x;
    struct MyStruct* previous;
    struct MyStruct* next;
};
```

Similarly, to declare a structure that will represent a node in the binary tree, we can write:

```
struct MyNode
{
    int x;
    struct MyNode* left;
    struct MyNode* right;
};
```

15.7 Structures as Function Arguments

We can use a structure as a function argument. The function argument is passed *by value*, meaning the function makes a copy of the arguments and continues to work with that copy. The original argument is unaffected by function. To pass the structure by value, we write:

```
#include <stdio.h>

struct MyStruct
{
    char c;
    int x;
    double d;
};

void myfunction(struct MyStruct myparameter)
{
    printf("Member c has a value of %c\n", myparameter.c);
    printf("Member x has a value of %d\n", myparameter.x);
    printf("Member d has a value of %f\n", myparameter.d);
}

int main(void)
{
    struct MyStruct s = {'a', 123, 456.789};
    myfunction(s);
}
```

Output:

```
Member c has a value of a
Member x has a value of 123
Member d has a value of 456.789000
```

This example uses a function that accepts the structure as a parameter. We have one function parameter called myparameter of type struct MyStruct. In the main program, we initialize a variable of type struct MyStruct called s. Then we pass this variable as an argument to our myfunction function, which prints out its member values.

To avoid typing a lengthy struct MyStruct type name, we can use a typedef to create an alias and shorten the declaration:

```c
#include <stdio.h>

typedef struct
{
    char c;
    int x;
    double d;
} MyStruct;

void myfunction(MyStruct myparameter)
{
    printf("Member c has a value of %c\n", myparameter.c);
    printf("Member x has a value of %d\n", myparameter.x);
    printf("Member d has a value of %f\n", myparameter.d);
}

int main(void)
{
    MyStruct s = {'a', 123, 456.789};
    myfunction(s);
}
```

Output:

```
Member c has a value of a
Member x has a value of 123
Member d has a value of 456.789000
```

Instead of having to type the entire struct MyStruct type name in the declarations, we can now simply use the MyStruct name.

Let us now create a function that is of some structure type and returns a structure value. Function parameters represent the values for the structure members. Example:

```c
#include <stdio.h>

struct MyStruct
{
    char c;
    int x;
    double d;
};

struct MyStruct createStruct(char cparam, int xparam, double dparam)
{
    struct MyStruct temps;
    temps.c = cparam;
    temps.x = xparam;
    temps.d = dparam;
    return temps;
}

int main(void)
{
    struct MyStruct s;
    s = createStruct('c', 123, 456.789);
    printf("Member c has a value of %c\n", s.c);
    printf("Member x has a value of %d\n", s.x);
    printf("Member d has a value of %f\n", s.d);
}
```

Output:

```
Member c has a value of c
Member x has a value of 123
Member d has a value of 456.789000
```

Since a structure is a type, we can have a function of that (structure) type. Here, we created a function called createStruct of type struct MyStruct. The function accepts three parameters, which will be used to assign values to three structure members. The function body declares a temporary variable called temps of type struct MyStruct. We then assign the parameter values to this temporary structure variable and return the variable temps to our caller using the return temps; statement. In our main program, we declare a variable s of type struct MyStruct and assign it a value returned by a function call. We used arbitrary values of 'c', 123, 456.789 as function arguments.

When a structure gets large, it is better/more efficient to pass the pointer to a structure rather than a structure itself. Example:

```
#include <stdio.h>

struct MyStruct
{
    char c;
    int x;
    double d;
};

void printStruct(struct MyStruct *myparameter)
{
    printf("Member c has a value of %c\n", myparameter->c);
    printf("Member x has a value of %d\n", myparameter->x);
    printf("Member d has a value of %f\n", myparameter->d);
}

int main(void)
{
    struct MyStruct s = {'a', 123, 456.789};
    printStruct(&s);
}
```

Output:

```
Member c has a value of a
Member x has a value of 123
Member d has a value of 456.789000
```

Here, we defined a function called printStruct that accepts a pointer to a structure as a parameter. Since this function accepts a pointer type, we use an address of an existing variable &s as an argument, not the s itself.

CHAPTER 16

Unions

A union is a user-defined type whose members overlap in memory. Unlike a structure whose members occupy separate regions of memory, the union's members all occupy the same memory region. The size of the union is equal to the size of its largest field. When declaring a union, we use the following syntax:

```
union some_name
{
    type_name member_name_1;
    type_name member_name_2;
    // ...
};
```

To define and use a simple union having three fields, we write:

```
#include <stdio.h>

union MyUnion
{
    char c;
    int x;
    double d;
};

int main(void)
{
    union MyUnion u;
    u.c = 'A';
    printf("The union's char member value: %c\n", u.c);
    u.x = 123;
    printf("The union's int member value: %d\n", u.x);
```

© Slobodan Dmitrović 2024
S. Dmitrović, *Modern C for Absolute Beginners*, https://doi.org/10.1007/979-8-8688-0224-9_16

```
    u.d = 456.789;
    printf("The union's double member value: %f\n", u.d);
}
```

Output:

```
The union's char member value: A
The union's int member value: 123
The union's double member value: 456.789000
```

With unions, we can access only the last modified field. In this example, we set the c field to the value of `'A'` and then print/access it using the `printf` function. We did the same for x and d. Trying to access the field that was not the last one to be modified results in undefined behavior. Since all three members share the same memory, we cannot do `u.x = 123;` and then try to access `u.c` or `u.d`. We can only access the `u.x` since it was the last modified field. Unions can store the value of only one of the members at any given time.

CHAPTER 17

Conditional Expression

The following example uses the if-else statement to assign the value to our result variable based on some (x > 10) condition:

```c
#include <stdio.h>

int main(void)
{
    int x = 123;
    int result;
    if (x > 10)
    {
        result = 456;
    }
    else
    {
        result = 789;
    }
    printf("The result is: %d\n", result);
}
```

Output:

```
The result is: 456
```

The similar behavior can be achieved using the *conditional expression*, which has the following syntax:

```c
(condition) ? expression1 : expression2
```

© Slobodan Dmitrović 2024
S. Dmitrović, *Modern C for Absolute Beginners*, https://doi.org/10.1007/979-8-8688-0224-9_17

The conditional expression inspects the value of a condition. If the condition is true /
anything else than 0, the conditional expression returns the expression1. Otherwise, it
returns the expression2. The ?: is a ternary operator used in the syntax. The preceding
code example can be rewritten as:

```c
#include <stdio.h>

int main(void)
{
    int x = 123;
    int result;
    result = (x > 10) ? 456 : 789;
    printf("The result is: %d\n", result);
}
```

Output:

```
The result is: 456
```

The following example shows how we can use the conditional expression inside the
printf function:

```c
#include <stdio.h>

int main(void)
{
    int x = 123;
    printf("Conditional expression result: %d\n", (x > 10) ? 456 : 789);
}
```

Output:

```
Conditional expression result: 456
```

CHAPTER 18

Typedef

The typedef declaration creates a synonym for the existing type. We use the typedef to create an *alias name* for the existing type name. The usage is of the following syntax:

```
typedef some_type our_new_name;
```

To create a new synonym for the type int and, for example, call it MyInteger, we type:

```
typedef int MyInteger;
```

Now, we can use the new MyInteger alias in the same way we would use int. Example:

```
#include <stdio.h>

typedef int MyInteger;

int main(void)
{
    MyInteger x = 123;
    printf("The value is: %d\n", x);
}
```

Output:

```
The value is: 123
```

© Slobodan Dmitrović 2024
S. Dmitrović, *Modern C for Absolute Beginners*, https://doi.org/10.1007/979-8-8688-0224-9_18

We can also create an alias for a pointer type:

```c
#include <stdio.h>

typedef char* MyString;

int main(void)
{
    MyString s = "Hello World!";
    printf("The value is: %s\n", s);
}
```

Output:

```
The value is: Hello World!
```

To create an alias for a structure type, we write:

```c
#include <stdio.h>

typedef struct MyStruct MyStruct;

struct MyStruct
{
    char c;
    int x;
    double d;
};

int main(void)
{
    MyStruct s;
    printf("Variable s of type MyStruct declared.\n");
}
```

Output:

```
Variable s of type MyStruct declared.
```

Or we can opt for the equivalent, more widely used typedef struct {} MyStruct; approach:

```
#include <stdio.h>

typedef struct
{
    char c;
    int x;
    double d;
} MyStruct;

int main(void)
{
    MyStruct s;
    printf("Variable s of type MyStruct declared.\n");
}
```

Output:

```
Variable s of type MyStruct declared.
```

The alias MyStruct, in this case, has the same name as the structure tag, which is allowed. Now, instead of having to type the lengthy structure type called struct MyStruct, we simply type MyStruct.

Note   With structs, the entire struct MyStruct wording represents the type name. To avoid having to type the lengthy struct MyStruct name, we create a *type alias* using the typedef struct {} MyStruct; approach. Now our type is simply called MyStruct.

CHAPTER 19

Const Qualifier

To make the object a *read-only object*, we apply the const qualifier to its declaration. Once initialized, these objects become read-only, and we call them *constants*. Attempting to change their values results in a *compile-time error*. Let us write an example that defines a few simple constants:

```
#include <stdio.h>

int main(void)
{
    const char c = 'a';
    const int x = 123;
    const double d = 456.789;
    printf("We have defined three constants.\n");
    printf("Their values are: %c, %d, %.3f.\n", c, x, d);
}
```

Output:

```
We have defined three constants.
Their values are: a, 123, 456.789.
```

This example defines three constants of three different types: const char, const int, and const double. These three names are now constants, and they are *read-only*. From now on, any attempt to change their values will result in a compile-time error. Example:

© Slobodan Dmitrović 2024
S. Dmitrović, *Modern C for Absolute Beginners*, https://doi.org/10.1007/979-8-8688-0224-9_19

```
#include <stdio.h>

int main(void)
{
    const char c = 'a';
    const int x = 123;
    const double d = 456.789;
    c = 'b';     // compile-time error
    x = 124;     // compile-time error
    d = 457.789; // compile-time error
    printf("Defined three constants.\n");
    printf("Their values are: %c, %d, %.3f.\n", c, x, d);
}
```

In this example, we tried to change the values of the constant. This results in three compile-time errors similar to:

```
error: assignment of read-only variable 'c'
error: assignment of read-only variable 'x'
error: assignment of read-only variable 'd'
```

We can also apply a const qualifier to pointer types. But with pointers, we have two things: a pointer variable itself and a pointed-to object. To make a pointer variable read-only, we put the const qualifier after the type name using the some_type* const p syntax:

```
#include <stdio.h>

int main(void)
{
    int x = 123;
    int *const p = &x; // constant pointer
    printf("Defined a constant pointer.\n");
    printf("Pointer value is: %p\n", (void *)p);
    printf("Pointed-to object value is: %d\n", *p);
}
```

Output:

```
Defined a constant pointer.
Pointer value is: 0x7fff8cb8dc7c
Pointed-to object value is: 123
```

If we now try to change the value of a pointer, for example, using a p = NULL;, we get a compile-time error as p is a constant.

To make a pointed-to object a read-only object, we place the const qualifier before the pointer type name using the const some_type* syntax. Example:

```
#include <stdio.h>

int main(void)
{
    int x = 123;
    const int *p = &x; // constant pointed-to object
    printf("Defined a constant, pointed-to object.\n");
    printf("Pointer value is: %p\n", (void *)p);
    printf("Pointed-to object value is: %d\n", *p);
}
```

Output:

```
Defined a constant, pointed-to object.
Pointer value is: 0x7ffdce8d2cac
Pointed-to object value is: 123
```

If we now attempt to change a pointed-to object's value using a *p = 456;, we get a compile-time error as *p is a constant. This only makes the pointed-to object a read-only object when trying to modify its value via the dereferenced pointer. However, we are still able to change the value of that object using the variable x.

To make the pointer and the pointed-to object read-only, we place the const qualifier before and after the pointer type name using the const some_type* const syntax. Example:

```
#include <stdio.h>

int main(void)
{
    int x = 123;
    const int *const p = &x; // constant pointer and constant pointed-
    to object
    printf("Defined a constant pointer and a constant pointed-to
    object.\n");
    printf("Pointer value is: %p\n", (void *)p);
    printf("Pointed-to object value is: %d\n", *p);
}
```

Output:

```
Defined a constant pointer and a constant pointed-to object.
Pointer value is: 0x7ffd3c1cc12c
Pointed-to object value is: 123
```

If we now try to change the pointer value or the pointed-to object value, we get a compile-time error.

Similar to making variables constant, we can also have constant function parameters. Declaring a constant function parameter ensures the function cannot alter the parameter's value. An example of a function having a constant parameter:

```
#include <stdio.h>

void myfunction(const int *myparam)
{
    printf("Using a constant function parameter.\n");
    printf("Pointer value is: %p\n", (void *)myparam);
    printf("Pointed-to object value is: %d\n", *myparam);
}
```

```
int main(void)
{
    int x = 123;
    int *p = &x;
    myfunction(p);
}
```

Output:

```
Using a constant function parameter.
Pointer value is: 0x7fff605a268c
Pointed-to object value is: 123
```

This example defines a function that declares a constant parameter called myparam. Having a constant parameter ensures the function does not alter the parameter value.

Please note that the const qualifier is a *type qualifier*, so int and const int should be treated as two different types.

CHAPTER 20

Enumerations

Enumerations are types whose values are symbolic names. These names have underlying integral values. To declare an enumeration type, we use the following syntax:

```
enum MyEnumName { Some_Enum_Name1, Some_Enum_Name2 };
```

We give the enum a name and then provide a list of enumerator names inside the curly braces. These names are also called *enumerators* or *enumeration constants*. The first enumerator has an underlying value of 0. The subsequent enumerators have the value of 2, 3, … To declare an enum type and a variable of that type, we write:

```c
#include <stdio.h>

int main(void)
{
    enum MyEnum
    {
        FIRST,
        SECOND,
        THIRD
    };
    enum MyEnum myEnumVar;
    myEnumVar = SECOND;
    printf("Declared an enum. Setting the value to: %d\n", myEnumVar);
}
```

Output:

```
Declared an enum. Setting the value to: 1
```

© Slobodan Dmitrović 2024
S. Dmitrović, *Modern C for Absolute Beginners*, https://doi.org/10.1007/979-8-8688-0224-9_20

This example declares an enum type called MyEnum. The type has three symbolic constants we named FIRST, SECOND, and THIRD. These enumerators have underlying values of 0, 1, and 2, respectively. We then declare a variable of this type and assign it a SECOND value. When declaring a variable of enum type, we must also use the enum word as in enum MyEnum myEnumVar;.

We can also explicitly specify the underlying enum values. An example where we declare an enum whose first enumerator starts from 3:

```c
#include <stdio.h>

int main(void)
{
    enum Days
    {
        WEDNESDAY = 3,
        THURSDAY,
        FRIDAY
    };

    enum Days myDays;
    myDays = FRIDAY;
    printf("Declared an enum. Setting the value to: %d\n", myDays);
}
```

Output:

```
Declared an enum. Setting the value to: 5
```

In this example, we explicitly specify that the first enum has a value of 3 and subsequent enums have a value of 4 and 5, respectively.

Another way to declare a variable of enum type is to put the variable name after the enum declaration. Example:

```c
#include <stdio.h>

int main(void)
{
    enum Days
```

```
    {
        WEDNESDAY = 3,
        THURSDAY,
        FRIDAY
    } myDays;

    myDays = FRIDAY;
    printf("Declared an enum. Setting the value to: %d\n", myDays);
}
```

Output:

Declared an enum. Setting the value to: 5

Enums can also be declared in a global scope and can be converted to integers. Example:

```
#include <stdio.h>

enum Lights
{
    RED,
    YELLOW,
    GREEN
};

int main(void)
{
    enum Lights myLights;
    myLights = GREEN;
    int x = myLights;
    printf("Converting an enum to integer. The value is: %d\n", x);
}
```

Output:

Converting an enum to integer. The value is: 2

In this example, we declared an enum type inside a global/file scope outside the function main. We then used a variable of enum type to initialize another variable of an int type.

In short, enums are a convenient way of representing a state using symbolic names.

CHAPTER 21

Function Pointers

Functions are not variables, but we can still have *pointers to functions* or *function pointers*. For example, if we have a simple function:

```
void myfunction()
{
    printf("Hello World from a function.\n");
}
```

If we want to declare a function pointer to this function, we write:

```
void (*fp)();
```

We need to enclose the function pointer name in parentheses due to * operator precedence.

The return type of a function pointer matches the function's return type, which, in our case, is void. To assign a function to our function pointer, we write:

```
fp = myfunction;
```

Now, we can invoke a function using a function pointer:

```
#include <stdio.h>

void myfunction()
{
    printf("Hello World from a function.\n");
}
```

© Slobodan Dmitrović 2024
S. Dmitrović, *Modern C for Absolute Beginners*, https://doi.org/10.1007/979-8-8688-0224-9_21

```
int main(void)
{
    void (*fp)();
    fp = myfunction;
    fp();
}
```

Output:

```
Hello World from a function.
```

Suppose our function has one parameter of type char*, for example. In that case, we modify the function pointer declaration to include that argument's type:

```
#include <stdio.h>

void myfunction(char *arg)
{
    printf("%s\n", arg);
}

int main(void)
{
    void (*fp)(char *);
    fp = myfunction;
    fp("This is a function argument.");
}
```

Output:

```
This is a function argument.
```

Similarly, if a function has multiple parameters, we match those parameters' types in the function pointer declaration as well:

```
#include <stdio.h>

void myfunction(char *arg1, int arg2)
{
```

```
      printf("%s %d\n", arg1, arg2);
}

int main(void)
{
      void (*fp)(char *, int);
      fp = myfunction;
      fp("The value of an int argument is:", 123);
}
```

Output:

```
The value of an int argument is: 123
```

Please note that we do not need to free the function pointer explicitly.

CHAPTER 22

Exercises

22.1 Structure Definition

Write a program that defines a simple structure called `Person`. The structure has the `char*`, `int`, and `double` fields. Declare a variable of this structure type inside the `main` and assign values to each member field. Print out the values:

```c
#include <stdio.h>

struct Person
{
    char *name;
    int age;
    double salary;
};

int main(void)
{
    struct Person o;
    o.name = "John Doe";
    o.age = 35;
    o.salary = 2500.00;
    printf("Name: %s\n", o.name);
    printf("Age: %d\n", o.age);
    printf("Salary: %.2f\n", o.salary);
}
```

© Slobodan Dmitrović 2024
S. Dmitrović, *Modern C for Absolute Beginners*, https://doi.org/10.1007/979-8-8688-0224-9_22

Output:

```
Name: John Doe
Age: 35
Salary: 2500.00
```

22.2 Structure Typedef Alias

Write a program that defines a typedef alias for the structure type called TPerson. The structure has the char*, int, and double fields. Declare a variable of this structure type inside the main and assign values to each member field. Print out the values:

```c
#include <stdio.h>

typedef struct
{
    char *name;
    int age;
    double salary;
} TPerson;

int main(void)
{
    TPerson o;
    o.name = "Sample Name";
    o.age = 35;
    o.salary = 2500.00;
    printf("Name: %s\n", o.name);
    printf("Age: %d\n", o.age);
    printf("Salary: %.2f\n", o.salary);
}
```

Output:

```
Name: Sample Name
Age: 35
Salary: 2500.00
```

22.3 Structure Initialization

Write a program that defines a structure. The structure has the char[ ], int, and double fields. Declare and initialize a variable of this structure type. Print out the values:

```c
#include <stdio.h>

typedef struct
{
    char name[50];
    int age;
    double salary;
} TPerson;

int main(void)
{
    TPerson o = {"John Doe", 25, 2500.00};
    printf("Name: %s\n", o.name);
    printf("Age: %d\n", o.age);
    printf("Salary: %.2f\n", o.salary);
}
```

Output:

```
Name: John Doe
Age: 25
Salary: 2500.00
```

22.4 Pointers to Structures

Write a program that defines an arbitrary structure. Create an instance of this structure in the main program. Define a pointer variable that points at this structure instance. Print the object fields using a pointer:

```c
#include <stdio.h>

typedef struct
{
```

```
        char arr[50];
        int x;
        double d;
} TMyStruct;

int main(void)
{
        TMyStruct o = {"Hello World from a struct!", 123, 456.789};
        TMyStruct *p = &o;
        printf("Array field: %s\n", p->arr);
        printf("Integer field: %d\n", p->x);
        printf("Double field: %f\n", p->d);
}
```

Output:

```
Array field: Hello World from a struct!
Integer field: 123
Double field: 456.789000
```

22.5 Unions

Write a program that defines a union type using a typedef alias. The union has the fields of type char*, int, and double. Create an instance of this union in the main program. Modify and print each of the fields. Ensure that only the last modified field is accessed:

```
#include <stdio.h>

typedef union
{
        char *arr;
        int x;
        double d;
} TMyUnion;
```

```
int main(void)
{
    TMyUnion u;
    u.arr = "Hello World from a union!";
    printf("Union's array field: %s\n", u.arr);
    u.x = 123;
    printf("Union's integer field: %d\n", u.x);
    u.d = 456.789;
    printf("Union's double field: %f\n", u.d);
}
```

Output:

```
Union's array field: Hello World from a union!
Union's integer field: 123
Union's double field: 456.789000
```

22.6 Constants and Pointers

Write a program that defines a constant name, a constant pointer, and a constant pointee. The values are arbitrary:

```
#include <stdio.h>

int main(void)
{
    // const name
    const int x = 123;
    // const pointer, can not use: p = "Something else";
    char *const p = "Hello World";
    int y = 456;
    // const pointee, can not use: *p2 = 789;
    const int *p2 = &y;
    printf("Constant name: %d\n", x);
    printf("Constant pointer: %p\n", (void *)p);
    printf("Constant pointee: %d\n", *p2);
}
```

Output:

```
Constant name: 123
Constant pointer: 0x5570c62d0004
Constant pointee: 456
```

22.7 Constant Function Parameters

Write a program that defines a function having constant parameters. Invoke the function in the main program. Function parameter types and argument values are arbitrary:

```c
#include <stdio.h>

double myfunction(const int a, const double b)
{
    return a / b;
}

int main(void)
{
    int x = 123;
    double y = 456.789;
    double result = myfunction(x, y);
    printf("The function call result is: %f\n", result);
}
```

Output:

```
The function call result is: 0.269271
```

22.8 Enums

Write a program that defines an enum type called MyEnum. The enum has three enumerators representing arbitrary colors. Create an object of that enum and use it in a switch statement. Use the switch statement to print the value of an enum object:

```
#include <stdio.h>

enum MyEnum
{
    RED,
    YELLOW,
    GREEN
};

int main(void)
{
    enum MyEnum myenum;
    myenum = GREEN;
    switch (myenum)
    {
    case RED:
        printf("The color is red.\n");
        break;
    case YELLOW:
        printf("The color is yellow.\n");
        break;
    case GREEN:
        printf("The color is green.\n");
        break;
    default:
        printf("None of the above.\n");
        break;
    }
}
```

Output:

```
The color is green.
```

22.9 Pointers to Functions

Write a program that defines two functions. The types of functions and the types of parameters are arbitrary. Define function pointers to these two functions. Invoke the functions using function pointers:

```c
#include <stdio.h>

void printmessage(const char *arg)
{
    printf("%s\n", arg);
}

double division(int a, double b)
{
    return a / b;
}

int main(void)
{
    void (*fp1)(const char *);
    double (*fp2)(int, double);
    fp1 = printmessage;
    fp2 = division;
    fp1("This is the function call through a function pointer.");
    double result = fp2(123, 456.789);
    printf("The result obtained through a function pointer is: %f\n",
    result);
}
```

Output:

```
This is the function call through a function pointer.
The result obtained through a function pointer is: 0.269271
```

CHAPTER 23

Preprocessor

When we compile our program, many things are happening in sequence, and here, we will take a look at the three major steps:

- Preprocessing

- Compilation

- Linking

The *preprocessing* is a process in which the preprocessor modifies the content of our source file(s) in various ways. The compiler then *compiles* the source code and turns it into *object files*. The linker then *links* the object files together and produces an executable file or a library.

When we start the compilation process, a preprocessor tool modifies our file's source code before the compilation process begins. It does so by using various *preprocessor directives*. Directives start with a # sign and do not end with a semicolon. Directives are not statements. Although they appear as statements to us humans when we read the code, they are instructions to a preprocessor on how to modify our source code's content before the compilation phase begins. Remember the use of #include <stdio.h>? That is also a preprocessor directive. Let us start with the #include directive.

23.1 #include

The #include directive includes/inserts the content of a specified file into our source file. The files to be included are usually header files with the extension of (.h). The directive is of the following syntax:

```
#include <filename.ext>
and:
#include "filename.ext"
```

© Slobodan Dmitrović 2024
S. Dmitrović, *Modern C for Absolute Beginners*, https://doi.org/10.1007/979-8-8688-0224-9_23

When we need to include the file that is part of the standard library, we enclose the file name in angle brackets < >. This tells the compiler to search for the file in a predetermined standard-library location.

We can create our own header files and refer to them as *user-defined header files*. To include the user-defined header, we enclose the file name with double quotes (" "). Now, the compiler searches for the file in the same directory where our source code file is. If it cannot find it there, it also searches in the standard library location.

Let us create an example that includes several standard-library files:

```c
#include <stdio.h>
#include <stdlib.h>
#include <string.h>

int main(void)
{
    printf("Included several standard-library headers.\n");
}
```

Output:

```
Included several standard-library headers.
```

This example includes multiple standard-library header files. This enables us to use the facilities declared in those header files in our main program. We discuss the standard library in greater detail in Part 2.

Let us now create a header file of our own, name it *myheaderfile.h*, and place it in the same folder where our *source.c* file is. The header file can be empty for now, as we are only using it to demonstrate how to include the user-defined header file into our source file. The content of our *source.c* file is:

```c
#include <stdio.h>        // standard library header file
#include "myheaderfile.h" // user-defined header file

int main(void)
{
    printf("Included one standard-library header and one user-defined
    header file.\n");
}
```

Output:

```
Included one standard-library header and one user-defined header file.
```

The first #include directive includes the standard-library header file called *stdio.h*, and the second #include directive includes our user-defined header file called *myheaderfile.h* into our *source.c* file.

So, instead of copying the header file content by hand and then pasting it into our source file, we simply use the #include directive, which does this job for us.

23.2 #define

The #define directive creates a macro name. It is of the following syntax:

```
#define some_identifier replacement_text
```

The #define directive replaces an *identifier* with the *replacement_text* in our source code. The preprocessor *replaces* all occurrences of *some_identifier_name* with the *some_replacement_text* in our source code when the compilation begins. Example:

```
#include <stdio.h>
#define MAX 100

int main(void)
{
    printf("Symbolic identifier MAX is: %d\n", MAX);
}
```

Output:

```
Symbolic identifier MAX is: 100
```

This example defines a symbolic name MAX that we can use in our program. Every occurrence of this identifier gets replaced by the text 100. The macro identifier name is all uppercase by convention. We can use this macro as an initializer for our variables:

```
#include <stdio.h>
#define MAX 100

int main(void)
{
    int x = MAX;
    printf("The value of x is: %d\n", x);
}
```

Output:

```
The value of x is: 100
```

Or in array declarations and loops:

```
#include <stdio.h>
#define ARRAY_ELEMENTS 3

int main(void)
{
    int arr[ARRAY_ELEMENTS];
    arr[0] = 10;
    arr[1] = 20;
    arr[2] = 30;
    for (int i = 0; i < ARRAY_ELEMENTS; i++)
    {
        printf("%d\n", arr[i]);
    }
}
```

Output:

```
10
20
30
```

Remember, the identifier ARRAY_ELEMENTS here is just a text macro that gets *expanded* to some other text when the compilation begins. The name itself is not a variable/object that occupies a memory. The preprocessor simply replaces every occurrence of ARRAY_ELEMENTS with 100 when the compilation begins. It is more meaningful to us to use some symbolic name ARRAY_ELEMENTS instead of a magic number 100.

We can also define a macro that represents a character value:

```
#include <stdio.h>
#define MY_NEW_LINE '\n'
#define MY_SPACE ' '

int main(void)
{
    printf("This example%cuses %cmacros.", MY_SPACE, MY_NEW_LINE);
}
```

Output:

```
This example uses
macros.
```

23.3 #undef

When we no longer need a macro or we want to redefine a macro, we use the #undef directive to *undefine* a macro name. An example where we undefine a macro:

```
#include <stdio.h>
#define MY_MAX 123

int main(void)
{
    int x = MY_MAX;
    printf("The value is: %d\n", x);
#undef MY_MAX
    printf("Macro undefined. The name MY_MAX no longer exists.\n");
}
```

Output:

```
The value is: 123
Macro undefined. The name MY_MAX no longer exists.
```

Before we can *redefine* a macro, we must first *undefine* it. Example:

```c
#include <stdio.h>
#define MY_MAX 123

int main(void)
{
    int x = MY_MAX;
    printf("The value is: %d\n", x);
#undef MY_MAX
    printf("Macro undefined. The name MY_MAX no longer exists.\n");
#define MY_MAX 456
    printf("Macro MY_MAX redefined and exists again.\n");
    x = MY_MAX;
    printf("The value is: %d\n", x);
}
```

Output:

```
The value is: 123
Macro undefined. The name MY_MAX no longer exists.
Macro MY_MAX redefined and exists again.
The value is: 456
```

This example *redefines* a MY_MAX macro with a new value. The workflow was as follows: define a macro, use it, undefine it, and then define it again with a new value. The compiler would issue a warning if we left out the #undef step.

23.4 Conditional Compilation

We can also compile some parts (portions, sections, areas) of the source code and exclude others. We do so by utilizing a few *conditional directives.*

23.4.1 #if

The #if directive is of the following syntax:

```
#if some_condition_that_is_constant_expression
      Our source code
#endif
```

The portion of the code surrounded by the #if and #endif directives will get compiled if the condition is true.

The #if directive checks the value of a condition (that is a constant expression). It marks the beginning of the source code that we want to compile. Every #if directive is matched by an #endif directive. The #endif directive marks the end of the #if block, which is the end of the source code chunk we want to compile. If the condition checked by the #if directive is true, the portion of the code gets compiled. If not, it is skipped. Example:

```
#include <stdio.h>
#define MY_FLAG 123

int main(void)
{
#if MY_FLAG < 123
      printf("This portion of the code (A)\n");
      printf("will not get compiled.\n");
#endif
      printf("This portion of the code (B)\n");
      printf("Will get compiled.\n");
}
```

Output:

```
This portion of the code (B)
Will get compiled.
```

Here, we define a macro called MY_FLAG that expands to a constant expression of 123. We then use the #if directive to check if the macro expression *is less* than 123. Since it is not, the portion of the code surrounded by the #if and #endif directives will not be compiled – it will be skipped.

We can also include additional #else and #elseif directives inside the #if #endif block to make multiple branches or check for multiple conditions. Example:

```c
#include <stdio.h>
#define MY_FLAG 123

int main(void)
{
#if MY_FLAG < 123
    printf("This portion of the code (A)\n");
    printf("will not get compiled.\n");
#elif MY_FLAG == 123
    printf("This portion of the code (B)\n");
    printf("will get compiled.\n");
#else
    printf("This portion of the code (C)\n");
    printf("will also be skipped.\n");
#endif
}
```

Output:

```
This portion of the code (B)
Will get compiled.
```

In this example, only the source code portion in the #elif part/branch will be compiled because only the MY_FLAG == 123 condition evaluates to true.

23.4.2 #ifdef

The #ifdef directive checks if a macro name is defined. The directive is of the following syntax:

```
#ifdef macro_name
      Our source code
#endif
```

We use the #ifdef directive to conditionally compile parts of the source code by checking if some macro was previously defined. If true, the source code portion gets compiled. Example:

```
#include <stdio.h>
#define MY_MACRO

int main(void)
{
#ifdef MY_MACRO
      printf("This portion of the code (A)\n");
      printf("will get compiled.\n");
#endif
#ifdef NON_EXISTING_MACRO
      printf("This portion of the code (B)\n");
      printf("will not get compiled.\n");
#endif
}
```

Output:

```
This portion of the code (A)
will get compiled.
```

Explanation: In this example, we define a macro called MY_MACRO using the #define MY_MACRO statement (without specifying the replacement value, it is okay; we can do that with #define). Then, we check if this macro is defined with the #ifdef MY_MACRO preprocessor command. Since it is defined, the source code chunk gets compiled.

Then, we proceed to check if some nonexistent macro called NON_EXISTING_MACRO is defined using the #ifdef NON_EXISTING_MACRO command. It is not, as there is no previously defined macro with the name of NON_EXISTING_MACRO, and the following source code gets excluded from the compilation.

23.4.3 #ifndef

The #ifndef directive checks if a macro name *is not defined*. The directive uses the following syntax:

```
#ifndef macro_name
    Our source code
#endif
```

This directive checks if a given macro name is *not defined* and, if that is the case, compiles the portion of source code ending with a #endif directive. Example:

```
#include <stdio.h>
#define MY_MACRO
int main(void)
{
#ifndef MY_MACRO
    printf("This portion of the code (A)\n");
    printf("will not get compiled.\n");
#endif
#ifndef NON_EXISTING_MACRO
    printf("This portion of the code (B)\n");
    printf("will get compiled.\n");
#endif
}
```

Output:

```
This portion of the code (B)
will get compiled.
```

This example defines a macro called MY_MACRO and then checks if this macro is *not* defined. Since the macro is defined earlier, the portion of the source code is skipped and not compiled.

The example then checks if a NON_EXISTING_MACRO is not defined. This is true – the macro, indeed, is not defined, and the source code that follows gets compiled.

We can utilize this directive to define a macro in case it was not already defined. Example:

```
#include <stdio.h>

int main(void)
{
#ifndef MY_MACRO
#define MY_MACRO
    printf("Macro defined.\n");
#endif
}
```

Output:

```
Macro defined.
```

This example checks if MY_MACRO is not defined. Since it is not, we continue and define it in the code that follows. This code is also referred to as a *code guard*, often used in header files to avoid multiple file inclusions. We discuss code guards in more detail in later chapters.

23.5 Built-In Macros

There are built-in macros we can use. For example, the __LINE__ built-in macro gives us the line number of the statement in which the macro is used:

```
#include <stdio.h>

int main(void)
{
      printf("The current source code line is: %d\n", __LINE__);
      printf("This statement is on line: %d\n", __LINE__);
}
```

Output:

```
The current source code line is: 5
This statement is on line: 6
```

The __FILE__ macro gives us (expands to) the name of the source code file:

```
#include <stdio.h>

int main(void)
{
      printf("This source code file is called: %s\n", __FILE__);
}
```

Output:

```
This source code file is called: source2.c
```

There are also __TIME__ and __DATE__ macros that expand to the time and date the preprocessor is used. Another built-in macro is the __STDC_VERSION__ macro that expands to a constant integer value representing the C standard used for compilation.

The __func__ string returns the name of the calling function. Example:

```
#include <stdio.h>

void myfunction()
{
      printf("This function's name is: %s\n", __func__);
}
```

```
int main(void)
{
    myfunction();
}
```

Output:

```
This function's name is: myfunction
```

23.6 Function-Like Macros

There are more complex macros that can accept arguments. These are called *function-like macros*. We invoke these macros the same way we call the functions.

Let us write a simple function-like macro that accepts two arguments and expands into a text that represents the sum of these two arguments:

```
#include <stdio.h>
#define MY_SUM(x, y) ((x) + (y))

int main(void)
{
    int mysum = MY_SUM(10, 20);
    printf("The result is: %d\n", mysum);
}
```

Output:

```
The result is: 30
```

This example defines a function-like macro that has two parameters x and y. The macro then *expands* into a ((x) + (y)) text that uses the same arguments. We used *extra parentheses* around parameters in the macro expansion to avoid any operator precedence issues. In the main program, we call this macro the same way we would call a function, and we provide two arbitrary arguments 10 and 20. At that point, the preprocessor substitutes the MY_SUM(10, 20) text with the ((10) + (20)) text. We can also say the macro MY_SUM(10, 20) *expands to* ((10) + (20)) text.

We can also use the preceding macro to sum two floating-point numbers:

```
#include <stdio.h>
#define MY_SUM(x, y) ((x) + (y))

int main(void)
{
    double mysum = MY_SUM(123.456, 789.101);
    printf("The result is: %.3lf\n", mysum);
}
```

Output:

```
The result is: 912.557
```

This example uses the same macro MY_SUM but with different types of arguments. Here, we used the macro to sum two arguments of type double.

While macro-like functions and macro-programming might look useful at first glance, they should be avoided for several reasons. Function-like macros are evaluated twice, do not preserve the type safety, are harder to read, and introduce unnecessary complexity.

Note   Prefer real functions to macro-like functions.

CHAPTER 24

Exercises

24.1 Define and Undefine a Macro

Write a program that defines, uses, and then undefines a macro. The macro names and their contents are arbitrary:

```c
#include <stdio.h>
// define the macro
#define MAX 999

int main(void)
{
    printf("Macro defined. The name MAX exists.\n");
    int x = MAX;
    printf("The variable assigned to macro has a value: %d\n", x);
// undefine the macro
#undef MAX
    printf("Macro undefined. The name MAX no longer exists.\n");
}
```

Output:

```
Macro defined. The name MAX exists.
The variable assigned to macro has a value: 999
Macro undefined. The name MAX no longer exists.
```

© Slobodan Dmitrović 2024
S. Dmitrović, *Modern C for Absolute Beginners*, https://doi.org/10.1007/979-8-8688-0224-9_24

24.2 Conditional Compilation

Write a program that defines an arbitrary macro called MY_CONDITIONAL_MACRO. Perform a conditional compilation based on existing and nonexisting macros. Utilize the #define, #ifdef, and #endif directives:

```
#include <stdio.h>

#define MY_CONDITIONAL_MACRO

int main(void)
{
#ifdef MY_CONDITIONAL_MACRO
    printf("This code will get compiled.\n");
#endif
#ifdef NON_EXISTING_MACRO
    printf("This code will not get compiled.\n");
#endif
}
```

   Output:

```
This code will get compiled.
```

24.3 Built-In Macros

Write a program that utilizes built-in macro names. The program prints out the statement's line number, the file name, the date when the file was created, the name of the function called, and the current C standard used:

```
#include <stdio.h>

void myfunction()
{
    printf("The name of the function called is: %s\n", __func__);
}
```

```
int main(void)
{
    printf("This statement is on line: %d\n", __LINE__);
    printf("The name of the source file is: %s\n", __FILE__);
    printf("The file was created on: %s\n", __DATE__);
    myfunction();
    printf("The C standard used is: %ld\n", __STDC_VERSION__);
}
```

Output:

```
This statement is on line: 10
The name of the source file is: source.c
The file was created on: Dec 18 2023
The name of the function called is: myfunction
The C standard used is: 201112
```

24.4 Function Macros

Write a program that defines two function-like macros. The first macro accepts two parameters and returns the lesser out of two values. The second macro also accepts two parameters and returns the greater out of two arguments. Call the macros in the main program:

```
#include <stdio.h>
#define MY_MIN(a, b) (((a) < (b)) ? (a) : (b))
#define MY_MAX(a, b) (((a) > (b)) ? (a) : (b))

int main(void)
{
    int x = 123;
    int y = 456;
    printf("The MY_MIN macro expands to: %d.\n", MY_MIN(x, y));
    printf("The MY_MAX macro expands to: %d.\n", MY_MAX(x, y));
}
```

Output:

```
The MY_MIN macro expands to: 123.
The MY_MAX macro expands to: 456.
```

CHAPTER 25

Dynamic Memory Allocation

So far, we have used pointers that point to regular, statically allocated variables. We used an address-of operator & to assign the address of an existing object to our pointer. Example:

```c
#include <stdio.h>

int main(void)
{
    int x = 123;
    int *p = &x;
    printf("The value of a pointed-to object is: %d\n", *p);
}
```

Output:

The value of a pointed-to object is: 123

We also showed how a pointer could point to an array:

```c
#include <stdio.h>

int main(void)
{
    int arr[] = {10, 20, 30, 40, 50};
    int *p = arr;
    printf("The first array element is: %d\n", *p);
}
```

© Slobodan Dmitrović 2024
S. Dmitrović, *Modern C for Absolute Beginners*, https://doi.org/10.1007/979-8-8688-0224-9_25

Output:

```
The first array element is: 10
```

Or a string constant:

```
#include <stdio.h>

int main(void)
{
    char *p = "Hello World!";
    printf("String constant: %s\n", p);
}
```

Output:

```
String constant: Hello World!
```

So far, we have used pointers only as another level of indirection for existing objects in memory.

There is another way we can utilize a pointer. During our program's execution, we can *dynamically* allocate the needed memory, use it, and free it. To do so, we use a few functions and a pointer. This chapter discusses the functions and techniques involved in dynamic memory allocation.

25.1 malloc

The malloc function allocates n bytes of memory from a system and returns a pointer to the newly allocated memory. The function has the following signature:

```
void* malloc(size_t size_in_bytes);
```

We need to include the <stdlib.h> header when using this function. To learn how to work with this function, we start with small, incomplete code examples and build in complexity until we have covered all the concepts.

To allocate memory for a single integer, we write:

```
#include <stdio.h>
#include <stdlib.h>

int main(void)
{
    int *p = malloc(sizeof(int));
    *p = 123;
    printf("The value is: %d\n", *p);
}
```

Output:

```
The value is: 123
```

Here, the malloc function allocates memory for a single integer. The pointer p now points at the beginning of the allocated memory block. We used the sizeof(int) expression to determine how many bytes we need for a single integer:

Figure 25-1. *A pointer pointing at a single, uninitialized block of memory representing a single uninitialized integer data object*

We have allocated space for a single integer. Assuming the size of the int is 4 bytes on our machine, we have allocated 4 bytes of memory:

Figure 25-2. *A pointer pointing at a single, uninitialized block of memory representing a single uninitialized integer data object. For example, a single uninitialized integer data object can occupy 4 bytes of memory*

189

When we dereference a pointer and assign a value of 123 to a pointed-to integer object, the image becomes:

Figure 25-3. *A pointer pointing at a single, initialized block of memory representing a single initialized integer data object whose value is 123*

If we inspect the individual bytes and their hexadecimal values and assume big-endian, the image might look like:

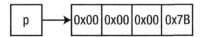

Figure 25-4. *A pointer pointing at a single, initialized block of memory representing a single initialized integer data object with underlying byte values*

If the allocation fails, the function returns NULL. It is good practice to check for the `malloc`'s return result using an `if` statement:

```
#include <stdio.h>
#include <stdlib.h>

int main(void)
{
    int *p = malloc(sizeof(int));
    if (p)
    {
        *p = 123;
        printf("The value is: %d\n", *p);
    }
}
```

Output:

```
The value is: 123
```

If we want to check if the result of memory allocation is NULL, we could write:

```
#include <stdio.h>
#include <stdlib.h>

int main(void)
{
    int *p = malloc(sizeof(int));
    if (p == NULL)
    {
        printf("Error allocating the memory. Exiting. ");
        return -1;
    }
    *p = 123;
}
```

Note   The previous examples are missing an important piece of code, and that is the call to a `free` function.

The expression `sizeof(int)` could have been rewritten as `sizeof *p` so that we do not repeat the type name. The type `size_t` represents an unsigned integer type often used for indexing and as a loop counter. It is also the return type of the `sizeof` operator.

Once allocated, we **must** manually release (free) the memory when we are done using it. We do so by using a `free()` function to which we pass the pointer returned by `malloc` as in `free(p);`. If we left out the `free` part, we would cause the so-called *memory leak*. This means that the dynamically allocated memory (using `malloc`) is never freed. We are leaking away available memory. It cannot be allocated again. So, the situation where we fail to release the dynamically allocated memory is called a *memory leak*. With that in mind, let us now write a complete example:

```
#include <stdio.h>
#include <stdlib.h>

int main(void)
{
    int *p = malloc(sizeof(int));
```

```
    if (p)
    {
        *p = 123;
        printf("The value is: %d\n", *p);
    }
    free(p);
}
```

Output:

```
The value is: 123
```

One school of thought says setting the pointer to NULL is good practice after we have freed the memory. While this might not be the case in modern C, we will provide a simple example:

```
#include <stdio.h>
#include <stdlib.h>

int main(void)
{
    int *p = malloc(sizeof(int));
    if (p)
    {
        *p = 123;
        printf("The value is: %d\n", *p);
    }
    free(p);
    p = NULL;
}
```

Output:

```
The value is: 123
```

Instead of using the sizeof(type_name) expression, we can also use the size of the dereferenced pointer, sizeof *p, which is the same. Example:

```c
#include <stdio.h>
#include <stdlib.h>

int main(void)
{
    int *p = malloc(sizeof *p);
    if (p)
    {
        *p = 123;
        printf("The value is: %d\n", *p);
    }
    free(p);
}
```

Output:

```
The value is: 123
```

Let us write an example that allocates space for five integers, sets the values of all five members, and frees the memory once done:

```c
#include <stdio.h>
#include <stdlib.h>

int main(void)
{
    int *p = malloc(5 * sizeof(int));
    if (p)
    {
        p[0] = 10;
        p[1] = 20;
        p[2] = 30;
        p[3] = 40;
        p[4] = 50;
        printf("Allocated an array of 5 integers.\n");
```

```
        // print out the array
        for (int i = 0; i < 5; i++)
        {
                printf("%d ", p[i]);
        }
    }
    free(p);
}
```

Output:

```
Allocated an array of 5 integers.
10 20 30 40 50
```

In this example, we allocated the space for five integers using the `malloc` function and the `5 * sizeof(int)` expression. This expression evaluates to the number of bytes capable of holding five integers. Then, we assign the values to each (array) element and print out the values.

In plain words, the workflow is as follows:

> Allocate (reserve/borrow) enough heap (free-store) memory from the system using a `malloc` function.
>
> Access and manipulate this memory using a pointer.
>
> Free the memory using a `free` function that will free (release/return) the previously allocated memory to the system so that it can be allocated again.

We can similarly allocate memory for a `char`:

```
#include <stdio.h>
#include <stdlib.h>

int main(void)
{
    char *p = malloc(sizeof(char));
    if (p)
```

```
    {
         *p = 'A';
         printf("The value is: %c\n", *p);
    }
    free(p);
}
```

Output:

```
The value is: A
```

To dynamically allocate a memory space for a structure, we write:

```
#include <stdio.h>
#include <stdlib.h>

typedef struct
{
     char c;
     int x;
     double d;
} MyStruct;

int main(void)
{
     MyStruct *p = malloc(sizeof(MyStruct));
     if (p)
     {
          p->c = 'A';
          p->x = 123;
          p->d = 456.789;
          printf("The value is: %c\n", p->c);
          printf("The value is: %d\n", p->x);
          printf("The value is: %f\n", p->d);
     }
     free(p);
}
```

Output:

```
The value is: A
The value is: 123
The value is: 456.789000
```

We declare a structure called MyStruct. The structure has three fields: char c, int x, and double d. We then allocate memory space for one data object of type MyStruct using a malloc function. The function returns a pointer p. We use this pointer to access our object in memory and populate the fields using the *member access through a pointer* -> operator. We print out the values and, finally, free the memory.

This struct-malloc combination is often used when creating data structures in memory, such as *linked lists*, *binary trees*, and similar.

25.2 calloc

The calloc function, defined inside the <stdlib.h> header, allocates space for an array of *n* objects of *some_size* size and initializes all bytes to zero. The memory block allocated with malloc is *uninitialized*. Bytes inside this block do not hold any meaningful values. If we need to allocate space that will be initialized with zeros, we use the calloc function instead. Unlike malloc, this function accepts two parameters and has the following signature:

```
void* calloc(size_t number_of_objects, size_t size_of_the_object)
```

To allocate space for a single integer and fill the allocated memory with zero(s), we write:

```
#include <stdio.h>
#include <stdlib.h>

int main(void)
{
    int *p = calloc(1, sizeof(int));
    if (p)
```

```
{
    printf("The initial value is: %d\n", *p);
}
free(p);
}
```

Output:

```
The initial value is: 0
```

The `calloc` function allocates the memory space needed and initializes all the allocated bytes with zeros:

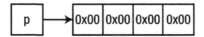

Figure 25-5. *A pointer pointing at a single, zero-initialized block of memory representing a single initialized integer data object with underlying byte values*

To allocate space for a single integer, fill the memory with zeros, and then change the value of the pointed-to data object in memory, we write:

```
#include <stdio.h>
#include <stdlib.h>

int main(void)
{
    int *p = calloc(1, sizeof(int)); // or (1, sizeof *p)
    if (p)
    {
        printf("The initial value is: %d\n", *p);
        *p = 123;
        printf("The new value is: %d\n", *p);
    }
    free(p);
}
```

197

Output:

```
The initial value is: 0
The new value is: 123
```

To allocate a space for an array of five integers, we write:

```c
#include <stdio.h>
#include <stdlib.h>

int main(void)
{
    int *p = calloc(5, sizeof(int));
    if (p)
    {
        printf("Initial values:\n");
        for (int i = 0; i < 5; i++)
        {
            printf("%d ", p[i]);
        }
        // set some values and print them out
        printf("\nNew values:\n");
        for (int i = 0; i < 5; i++)
        {
            p[i] = (i + 1) * 10;
            printf("%d ", p[i]);
        }
    }
    free(p);
}
```

Output:

```
Initial values:
0 0 0 0 0
New values:
10 20 30 40 50
```

25.3 realloc

Once we allocate space using malloc or calloc, and before we free that memory, we can grow or shrink that memory space using realloc. The function is defined inside the <stdlib.h> header file. The realloc function has the following signature:

```
void *realloc(void *pointer, size_t new_size_in_bytes)
```

The function takes two parameters. The first is the original pointer, and the second is the new memory size. The function returns a pointer to the newly allocated/reallocated memory block. For now, let us start with a simple yet *incomplete* example with error checking omitted:

```
#include <stdio.h>
#include <stdlib.h>

int main(void)
{
    int *p = malloc(sizeof(int));
    printf("Allocated %zu bytes.\n", sizeof *p);
    printf("Resizing allocated memory...\n");
    int *pnew = realloc(p, 10 * sizeof(int));
    printf("The memory block is now %zu bytes long.\n", 10 *
    sizeof(int));
}
```

Output:

```
Allocated 4 bytes.
Resizing allocated memory...
The memory block is now 40 bytes long.
```

By using the malloc function, this example allocates the memory block large enough to hold a single integer. It then assigns the address of this newly allocated memory block to pointer p. We then pass this pointer to the realloc function as a first argument. The second argument is the new size of a memory block. We want to expand the memory block to hold ten integers using the 10 * sizeof(int) expression.

Let us now write a complete example with error checking and properly placed free functions:

```c
#include <stdio.h>
#include <stdlib.h>

int main(void)
{
    int *p = malloc(sizeof(int));
    if (p)
    {
        printf("Allocated %zu bytes.\n", sizeof *p);
    }
    int *pnew = realloc(p, 10 * sizeof(int));
    if (pnew)
    {
        printf("Resizing allocated memory...\n");
        printf("The memory block is now %zu bytes long.\n",
        10 * sizeof(int));
        // reallocation successful, free the new pointer
        free(pnew);
    }
    else
    {
        // if reallocation fails, free the original pointer
        free(p);
    }
}
```

Output:

```
Allocated 4 bytes.
Resizing allocated memory...
The memory block is now 40 bytes long.
```

This example allocates space for a single integer and then reallocates/grows space so that it can hold ten integers. If reallocation succeeds, a new pointer is returned, and the old/original pointer is invalidated. We need to free this new/reallocated pointer using free(pnew). If reallocation fails, the function returns NULL and the old/original pointer is preserved, so we must free the original memory/pointer using free(p).

CHAPTER 26

Storage and Scope

Variables and data objects have certain properties such as *visibility*, *scope*, *storage*, and *lifetime*. These terms are all closely related, and here, we explain how they affect each other. We describe how names are visible to other names and how much time the data objects spend in memory.

26.1 Scope

When a variable (or a function) is declared, its name is only valid inside some portion/section of a source code. That section of a source code is called a *scope*. There are different kinds of scopes – local scope and global scope.

26.1.1 Local Scope

A function body starting with the { and ending with a } can be seen as a *local scope*. It is local to a function. Variables declared inside a function are visible and accessible only there. They are not accessible outside the function scope. We say those variables have a local scope. Example:

```
#include <stdio.h>

void myFunction(void)
{
    int x = 10; // x is a local variable, local to myFunction
    printf("Local scope variable x value: %d\n", x);
}
```

201

© Slobodan Dmitrović 2024
S. Dmitrović, *Modern C for Absolute Beginners*, https://doi.org/10.1007/979-8-8688-0224-9_26

```
int main(void)
{
    myFunction();
    int y = 20; // y is a local variable, local to main
    printf("Local scope variable y value: %d\n", y);
}
```

Output:

```
Local scope variable x value: 10
Local scope variable y value: 20
```

In this example, x is only visible and accessible within the myFunction and nowhere else. Similarly, y is only visible inside the function main and nowhere else.

26.1.2 Global Scope

When we look at the source file as a whole, we look at the *file scope* or a *global scope*. Everything declared inside a file scope is accessible and visible to everything else in the file scope that follows its declaration. Example:

```
#include <stdio.h>

int x = 123; // x has a global scope

int main(void)
{
    printf("X has a global scope and a value of: %d\n", x);
}
```

Output:

```
X has a global scope and a value of: 123
```

Variables and functions (names) inside a global scope are visible to names in a local scope. Example:

```c
#include <stdio.h>

int x = 123; // x has a global scope

void printX(void)
{
    // x is visible here because it has a global scope
    printf("X has a global scope and a value of: %d\n", x);
}

int main(void)
{
    printX();
}
```

Output:

```
X has a global scope and a value of: 123
```

Names in a local scope are not visible to names inside a global scope. Example:

```c
#include <stdio.h>

void myFunction(void)
{
    int x = 123; // x has a local scope
    // and is only visible in this block
}

// x is not visible here because it has a local scope
int main(void)
{
    // x is not visible here because it has a local scope
}
```

26.2 Storage

Every data object has its *storage* (occupied memory) and *storage duration* (the amount of time spent in memory). The storage duration determines the object's *lifetime*. The lifetime is a period of time (while our program is executing) during which the object occupies a memory. There are different kinds of storage durations. Here, we discuss a few.

26.2.1 Automatic Storage Duration

The default storage duration is *automatic* storage duration. This storage is allocated when the control flow enters the block in which the data object is declared. It is automatically deallocated when the control flow exits the block marked with }. Here, we can say the scope determines the lifetime of automatic storage variables. The variable goes out of scope when our program's control flow reaches the function's closing brace (}). It gets destroyed once it goes out of scope, and the previously occupied memory is automatically released. Automatic storage is often referred to as *stack memory*. Example:

```
#include <stdio.h>

int main(void)
{
    int x = 123; // x is declared here
    printf("Variable x has automatic storage and a value of: %d\n", x);
} // x goes out of scope here
```

Output:

```
Variable x has automatic storage and a value of: 123
```

Our variable x is declared inside a function main. This variable's storage is allocated when our program starts when the control flow enters the main's { brace and deallocated when the control flow hits the closing brace }. Here, the x goes out of scope, and the memory it occupies is automatically released. The same applies to user-defined functions:

```
#include <stdio.h>

void myFunction(void)
{
    int x = 123; // x is declared here
    printf("Variable x has automatic storage and a value of: %d\n", x);
} // x goes out of scope here

int main(void)
{
    myFunction();
}
```

Output:

```
Variable x has automatic storage and a value of: 123
```

26.2.2 Static Storage Duration

When we apply a static specifier to our variable declaration, our data object then has a static storage duration. It remains in memory *throughout the execution of our program.* Objects marked with static and objects declared in global/file scope have this duration. The static storage duration object is initialized only once and preserves its (last) value across multiple function calls. Example:

```
#include <stdio.h>

void myCounter(void)
{
    static int x = 10; // initialized only once
    x++;
    printf("Static variable value: %d\n", x);
}
```

```
int main(void)
{
    myCounter(); // x == 11
    myCounter(); // x == 12
    myCounter(); // x == 13
}
```

Output:

```
Static variable value: 11
Static variable value: 12
Static variable value: 13
```

Also, applying the static specifier to a variable or a function declared inside the global (file) scope makes them visible only inside that file/translation unit.

26.2.3 Allocated Storage Duration

Objects that are dynamically allocated have a so-called *allocated storage duration*. This means the storage for these objects dynamically changes throughout the execution of our program. We manually allocate memory for an object, use it, and then manually deallocate it when we no longer need it. Our responsibility is to manually and explicitly free the memory once we no longer need it. Objects with allocated storage duration do not automatically deallocate the memory once they go out of scope. We need to deallocate the memory manually. Example:

```
#include <stdio.h>
#include <stdlib.h>

int main(void)
{
    printf("Allocating an object...\n");
    int *p = malloc(sizeof(int));
    *p = 123;
    printf("Object with allocated storage has a value of: %d\n", *p);
    printf("Deallocating an object...\n");
```

```
        free(p);
        printf("Done.\n");
}
```

Output:

```
Allocating an object...
Object with allocated storage has a value of: 123
Deallocating an object...
Done.
```

Objects allocated with malloc, calloc, and realloc have an *allocated storage duration.*

CHAPTER 27

Exercises

27.1 Dynamic Memory Allocation

Write a program that dynamically allocates space for a double and space for an int using a dereferenced pointer size. Free the memory blocks afterward:

```c
#include <stdio.h>
#include <stdlib.h>
int main(void)
{
    // allocate space for a double
    double *p1 = malloc(sizeof(double));
    if (p1)
    {
        *p1 = 123.456;
        printf("The value is: %f\n", *p1);
    }
    free(p1);
    // allocate space for an int
    int *p2 = malloc(sizeof *p2);
    if (p2)
    {
        *p2 = 789;
        printf("The value is: %d\n", *p2);
    }
    free(p2);
}
```

© Slobodan Dmitrović 2024
S. Dmitrović, *Modern C for Absolute Beginners*, https://doi.org/10.1007/979-8-8688-0224-9_27

Output:

```
The value is: 123.456000
The value is: 789
```

27.2 Dynamic Memory Allocation: Arrays

Write a program that dynamically allocates space for an array of five doubles. Using a for loop, set and print out all the array elements. Free the memory afterward:

```c
#include <stdio.h>
#include <stdlib.h>

int main(void)
{
    // allocate space for 5 doubles
    double *p = malloc(5 * sizeof(double));
    if (p)
    {
        printf("The values are:\n");
        for (int i = 0; i < 5; i++)
        {
            p[i] = i;
            printf("%.2f ", p[i]);
        }
    }
    free(p);
}
```

Output:

```
The values are:
0.00 1.00 2.00 3.00 4.00
```

27.3 Dynamic Memory Resizing

Write a program that dynamically allocates memory for an array of five integers and then resizes the allocated block to hold an array of ten integers. Free the memory afterward:

```c
#include <stdio.h>
#include <stdlib.h>

int main(void)
{
    int *p = malloc(5 * sizeof(int));
    if (p)
    {
        printf("Allocated %zu bytes.\n", 5 * sizeof(int));
    }
    int *pnew = realloc(p, 10 * sizeof(int));
    if (pnew)
    {
        printf("Resizing allocated memory...\n");
        printf("The memory block is now %zu bytes long.\n", 10 *
        sizeof(int));
        // resizing successful, free the realloc pointer
        free(pnew);
    }
    else
    {
        // resizing fails, free the original pointer
        free(p);
    }
}
```

   Output:

```
Allocated 20 bytes.
Resizing allocated memory...
The memory block is now 40 bytes long.
```

27.4 Automatic and Allocated Storage

Write a program that defines two variables. The first variable will have an automatic storage duration, and the second variable will have an allocated storage duration:

```c
#include <stdio.h>
#include <stdlib.h>

int main(void)
{
    int x = 123;
    printf("The variable with an automatic storage duration: %d\n", x);

    int *p = malloc(sizeof(int));
    printf("The variable with an allocated storage duration: %p\n",
    (void *)p);
    free(p); // p is manually freed here
} // x is automatically freed here
```

Output:

```
The variable with an automatic storage duration: 123
The variable with an allocated storage duration: 0x555fd1ec16b0
```

CHAPTER 28

Standard Input and Output

The C standard library provides functions allowing us to accept data/characters from the standard input and output data/characters to the *standard output*. The *standard input* is usually a keyboard. The *standard output* is typically a monitor/console window to which we output the data.

28.1 Standard Input

This chapter describes a few functions that allow us to accept data from the standard input/keyboard. Here, we mention the `scanf` and the `fgets` functions. Worth noticing is that these functions are not part of the language per se but rather a part of the standard library.

28.1.1 scanf

The `scanf` function allows us to accept the formatted data from the standard input and store it into a variable(s). The function is declared inside the `<stdio.h>` header and has the following signature:

```
int scanf(const char* format, …)
```

The function accepts the following arguments: *format specifiers* and *addresses of variables* that will store/hold the input data. The format specifier interprets/formats the data from the standard input. The addresses of variables are used for storing the read data. The function returns the number of successfully assigned variables or EOF on error.

© Slobodan Dmitrović 2024
S. Dmitrović, *Modern C for Absolute Beginners*, https://doi.org/10.1007/979-8-8688-0224-9_28

To accept a single character from a keyboard and store it in our char variable, we would use the %c format specifier and an address of a char variable:

```
#include <stdio.h>

int main(void)
{
        printf("Enter a single character: ");
        char mychar;
        scanf("%c", &mychar);
        printf("You entered: %c\n", mychar);
}
```

Output:

```
Enter a single character: a
You entered: a
```

To accept an integer number from a keyboard and store it in our int variable, we use the %d format specifier and the address of an int variable. Example:

```
#include <stdio.h>

int main(void)
{
        printf("Enter an integer number: ");
        int x;
        scanf("%d", &x);
        printf("You entered: %d\n", x);
}
```

Output:

```
Enter an integer number: 123
You entered: 123
```

To accept multiple values from the standard input, we can use multiple format specifiers separated by spaces and multiple addresses of variables separated by commas. For example, to accept an int and a double from a keyboard, we write:

```
#include <stdio.h>

int main(void)
{
    printf("Enter an integer and a double: ");
    int x;
    double d;
    scanf("%d %lf", &x, &d);
    printf("You entered: %d and %lf\n", x, d);
}
```

Output:

```
Enter an integer and a double: 123 456.789
You entered: 123 and 456.789000
```

Note   The scanf function does not perform bounds checking and can potentially cause a buffer overflow.

28.1.2 sscanf

The sscanf function reads from a character array buffer instead of a standard input. It stores the read data into a comma-separated list of variables based on the provided format specifiers. The function has the following syntax:

```
int sscanf ( const char * buffer, const char * format, ...);
```

To extract a character array buffer into separate variables, we write:

```
#include <stdio.h>

int main(void)
{
    char buff[50] = "A 123 456.789";
    char c;
    int x;
    double d;
    sscanf(buff, "%c %d %lf", &c, &x, &d);
    printf("The values are: %c, %d and %lf\n", c, x, d);
}
```

Output:

```
The values are: A, 123 and 456.789000
```

In this example, the character buffer of "A 123 456.789" is matched by a "%c %d %f" format descriptor inside the sscanf function. If the string in the buffer contained the comma-separated values of "A,123,456.789", we would match those with the "%c,%d,%f" specifier in the sscanf function.

28.1.3 fgets

When accepting a string, using a fgets function instead of scanf is better. The scanf can cause the so-called *buffer overflow*. A buffer overflow occurs when the number of characters read is greater than the buffer size. It occurs when trying to accept a string larger than the buffer size. The fgets function is safe in that regard and does not cause the mentioned error. The fgets function is defined inside the <stdio.h> header, accepts three parameters, and has the following signature:

```
char *fgets(char *str, int char_count, FILE *stream_name);
```

The fgets function reads the input/characters from the given stream and stores the read characters into a character array/buffer pointed to by str. The function stops reading the input when we press ENTER, when a new-line character is encountered in a stream. We pass in the stdin parameter representing our keyboard to read (accept an input) from a keyboard.

The following example reads the input from the keyboard and stores it in our character array. A simple example with error checking omitted:

```
#include <stdio.h>

int main(void)
{
    // error checking omitted
    printf("Enter a string: ");
    char str[10];
    fgets(str, 10, stdin);
    printf("You entered: %s\n", str);
}
```

Output:

```
Enter a string: Sample string
You entered: Sample st
```

This example accepts an input from the keyboard and stores it into an str buffer. It does so by accepting at most nine characters, reserving the tenth place for the null character '\0'. Any remaining characters are discarded.

We provide the pointer to buffer str, a simple array of ten characters. We then tell the fgets function how many characters it should accept: 10 (actually nine as the tenth place is reserved for null character). This number is often the same as the array size. Finally, with the third argument, we tell the function where to accept the input from, which is a keyboard in our case (represented by stdin).

If the function succeeds, it returns the pointer to the buffer we provided, str in our case. If it fails, the function returns NULL. Here is a full example with the error checking:

```
#include <stdio.h>

int main(void)
{
    printf("Enter a string: ");
    char str[10];
```

```
        if (fgets(str, 10, stdin) != NULL)
        {
                printf("You entered: %s\n", str);
        }
        else
        {
                printf("Failure. No characters are read.\n");
        }
}
```

Output:

```
Enter a string: Sample string
You entered: Sample st
```

28.2 Standard Output

This section describes the functions that allow us to write/output data to a *standard output stream*, which is our console window in most cases.

28.2.1 printf

The printf function sends/outputs a formatted string to standard output. It can read our variables, format them according to the format specifier, and place them in an output string. The function has the following signature:

```
int printf(const char *message, var1, var2...);
```

To output a simple string to our console window, we write:

```
#include <stdio.h>

int main(void)
{
        printf("This message ends with a new-line character.\n");
}
```

Output:

```
This message ends with a new-line character.
```

To output the values of our variables, we write:

```
#include <stdio.h>

int main(void)
{
    char c = 'A';
    int x = 123;
    double d = 456.789;
    printf("The values are: %c, %d, and %3.2lf\n", c, x, d);
}
```

Output:

```
The values are: A, 123, and 456.79
```

We used three different format specifiers, %c, %d, and %f, to format char, int, and double values. The format specifier describes how the content of our variable should be formatted for the output. The format specifier also acts as a placeholder for the values, a placeholder within the output string.

The format specifier can also include the length/the number of characters needed to output our value. For example, to output a double value of 123.456 using three character spaces for an integral part and two spaces for the fractional part, we use the %3.2f format specifier:

```
#include <stdio.h>

int main(void)
{
    double d = 123.456;
    printf("%3.2lf\n", d);
}
```

Output:

```
123.46
```

This example displays a rounded second decimal. The value of the variable remains unchanged.

The following list includes some of the most used *format specifiers*:

%c – Writes one character, used for type char

%s – Writes a string, used for char arrays

%d or %i – Writes (converts) an integer, used for types char, short, or int

%u – Used for unsigned char, unsigned short, or unsigned int

%ld – Outputs a long int

%f – Outputs a float or a double value into a decimal representation

%lf – Outputs a double value into a decimal representation

x – Writes a hexadecimal representation of char, short, or int

28.2.2 puts

This function simply writes a string and a new-line character to the standard output (a console window). The function is defined inside the <stdio.h> header and has the following syntax:

```
int puts(const char *message);
```

To use this function, we type:

```
#include <stdio.h>

int main(void)
{
    puts("This is a puts() message.");
}
```

Output:

```
This is a puts() message.
```

The function outputs a simple message to the standard output. It also adds an extra new-line character to the output string. This saves us from having to explicitly type the \n character at the end of our message.

28.2.3 fputs

Another function for writing to the output stream is fputs. The function writes the null-terminated string to the chosen output stream. This function is defined inside the <stdio.h> header and has the following signature:

```
int fputs(const char *message, FILE *stream_name);
```

To write to the standard output, we supply the message string and the stdout parameter for the *standard output*. Example:

```
#include <stdio.h>

int main(void)
{
    fputs("This is a fputs() message.\n", stdout);
}
```

Output:

```
This is a fputs() message.
```

28.2.4 putchar

The putchar function outputs/writes a character to the standard output. The function is declared inside a <stdio.h> header and has the following syntax:

```
int putchar (int ch);
```

To write a single character to the standard output, we use:

```c
#include <stdio.h>

int main(void)
{
        char c = 'A';
        putchar(c);
}
```

Output:

A

To print out a character array, one character at a time, without error checking, we write:

```c
#include <stdio.h>

int main(void)
{
        char arr[] = "Hello!";
        for (size_t i = 0; i < 7; i++)
        {
                putchar(arr[i]);
        }
}
```

Output:

Hello!

If the function fails to print the character, it returns an int value equal to EOF.

CHAPTER 29

File Input and Output

A file is an array of bytes, usually stored on mediums such as drives. We can write to and read from a file using a few C standard-library functions. The following sections explain the workflow and the functions used.

29.1 File Input

To be able to read from a file, we need to utilize a couple of functions. The workflow is as follows:

- Open a file for reading using the `fopen` function.

- Read a line of text from a file using the `fgets` function.

- Close the file using the `fclose` function when done.

Let us first create a text file called `myfile.txt` and fill it with arbitrary text. We then place the text file in the same folder as our executable. A simple example with error checking omitted:

```c
#include <stdio.h>

int main(void)
{
    char str[100];
    FILE *fp = fopen("myfile.txt", "r"); // open a file
    while (fgets(str, 100, fp) != NULL) // read line of text
    {
        printf("%s", str); // print the line of text
    }
    fclose(fp); // close the file
}
```

© Slobodan Dmitrović 2024
S. Dmitrović, *Modern C for Absolute Beginners*, https://doi.org/10.1007/979-8-8688-0224-9_29

Possible Output:

```
This is line no. 1
Sample text
Hello World!
```

The statement FILE *fp = fopen("myfile.txt", "r"); opens a file for reading using the fopen function. The fopen function returns a pointer to a file stream represented by a FILE * type. The function accepts two parameters. The first parameter is a *file name*, in our case "myfile.txt". The second parameter is a *read mode*, in our case "r", which specifies we are opening a file for reading.

Then, inside a loop, we read from a file, one line at a time, using the fgets function: while (fgets(str, 100, fp) != NULL).

Inside the while loop, we print out the read lines using the printf function. When we reach the end of the file, the fgets function returns NULL, and the while loop exits.

Finally, we close the file handle by using the fclose(fp); statement. All these functions are defined inside the <stdio.h> header.

To check if the file can be opened, we inspect the pointer's value using the if (!fp) expression. If it is NULL, the opening of a file failed, and we exit the program:

```c
#include <stdio.h>

int main(void)
{
    char str[100];
    FILE *fp = fopen("myfile.txt", "r"); // open a file for reading
    if (!fp)
    {
        printf("Error opening the file. Exiting...\n");
        return 1; // exit the program with an error
    }
    while (fgets(str, 100, fp) != NULL) // read line of text
    {
        printf("%s", str); // print line of text
    }
    fclose(fp); // close the file
}
```

Possible Output:

```
This is line no. 1
Sample text
Hello World!
```

29.2 File Output

To write to a file, we use several functions in a sequence. The workflow when writing to a file is as follows:

- Open a file for writing using the fopen function.

- Write to a file using the fprintf function.

- When done writing, close the file using the fclose function.

The following example creates a file named myfile.txt and writes a single line of text to it:

```c
#include <stdio.h>

int main(void)
{
    FILE *fp = fopen("myfile.txt", "w"); // open a file for writing
    fprintf(fp, "%s", "my line of text"); // write a line of text
    fclose(fp); // close the file
}
```

This statement opens/creates a file for writing: FILE *fp = fopen("myfile.txt", "w");. The fopen function returns a pointer to the file stream, which is our fp. We then use the fprintf function to write a single line of text to this stream/file. The fprintf function is similar to fprint but accepts one more parameter: our pointer to a file stream.

When done writing to a file, we need to close the file handle by passing a file pointer fp to our fclose function using the fclose(fp); statement.

To write two lines of text, we use the following example:

```c
#include <stdio.h>

int main(void)
{
    FILE *fp = fopen("myfile.txt", "w"); // open a file for writing
    fprintf(fp, "%s\n%s", "Line 1", "Line 2"); // write two lines
    fclose(fp); // close the file
}
```

CHAPTER 30

Exercises

30.1 Standard Input

Write a program that accepts two variables of type int and double from the standard input. Use the fgets function to store the input into a buffer. Use the sscanf function to extract the buffer into variables:

```c
#include <stdio.h>

int main(void)
{
    printf("Enter an int and a double and press <enter>: \n");
    char buffer[50];
    int x;
    double d;
    // read the input and store it in a buffer string
    if (fgets(buffer, 50, stdin) != NULL)
    {
        // read from a buffer string into our variables
        sscanf(buffer, "%d %lf", &x, &d);
        printf("You entered: %d and %f\n", x, d);
    }
    else
    {
        printf("Failure. No characters are read.\n");
    }
}
```

© Slobodan Dmitrović 2024
S. Dmitrović, *Modern C for Absolute Beginners*, https://doi.org/10.1007/979-8-8688-0224-9_30

Output:

```
Enter an int and a double and press <enter>:
123 456.789
You entered: 123 and 456.789000
```

When scanning a double using the sscanf function, we need to use the %lf format specifier. For type float, a simple %f would suffice.

30.2 Standard Output

Write a program that defines several variables of built-in types. Print the variables using the appropriate format specifiers inside the printf function:

```c
#include <stdio.h>

int main(void)
{
    char c = 'A';
    int x = 123;
    double d = 456.789;
    size_t size = sizeof(long);
    int *p = &x;
    long l = 12345678910L;
    char str[] = "Hello World!";
    printf("Type char: %c\n", c);
    printf("Type int: %d\n", x);
    printf("Type double: %f\n", d);
    printf("Type size_t: %zu\n", size);
    printf("Pointer type: %p\n", (void *)p);
    printf("Type long: %ld\n", l);
    printf("Character array: %s\n", str);
}
```

Output:

```
Type char: A
Type int: 123
Type double: 456.789000
Type size_t: 8
Pointer type: 0x7ffcc5acd424
Type long: 12345678910
Character array: Hello World!
```

CHAPTER 31

Header and Source Files

Our C source code can be divided into multiple files called *header files* and *source files*. These files are plain text files containing C source code. By convention, the header files have the .h extension, and source files have the .c extension. Other extensions are also possible.

Standard-library header files are included by surrounding the header name with angle brackets <> as in:

```
#include <stdio.h>
```

And user-defined header files are included by surrounding the header file name with double quotes:

```
#include "someheader.h"
```

In general, we can place variable and function declarations/interfaces in header files and the implementation/definitions in source files. In simple words, we declare things in header files, include that header file in the source files, and define things in source files. This way, we can organize the code and separate the declarations from the definitions.

When the compilation begins, the content of the included header is stitched together with the source file. This produces one source code file, the so-called *translation unit*. So, having the #include "someheader.h" is the same as manually typing the entire header file's content in our source file.

Having declarations in header files allows us to share these declarations with multiple source files. For example, let us create a header file titled *myutils.h* where we declare some function, for example:

```
#include <stdio.h>
void myFunction();
```

© Slobodan Dmitrović 2024
S. Dmitrović, *Modern C for Absolute Beginners*, https://doi.org/10.1007/979-8-8688-0224-9_31

Let us then create a source file called *myutils.c* where we include this header and define a function:

```
#include "myutils.h"

void myFunction()
{
    printf("Declared in a header file and defined in a source file.\n");
}
```

Finally, we include the *myutils.h* header in our main *source.c* file and call the function:

```
#include <stdio.h>
#include "myutils.h"

int main(void)
{
    myFunction();
}
```

Output:

```
Declared in a header file and defined in a source file.
```

To compile this program, we must compile all the source files:

```
gcc -Wall source.c myutils.c -std=c11 -pedantic && ./a.out
```

One final thing left to do is to have the *code guards* in the shared header file. Code guard is a macro that prevents the inclusion of the header file contents more than once. Now our *myutils.h* header looks like the following:

```
#ifndef MY_UTILS_H
#define MY_UTILS_H

#include <stdio.h>
void myFunction();

#endif
```

We still include our header file in multiple files using the `#include "myutils.h"` directive. But now, the code guards ensure that the header file source code is included only once when compiling multiple files. As before, we compile with:

```
gcc -Wall source.c myutils.c -std=c11 -pedantic && ./a.out
```

Alternatively, replace the `-std=c11` flag with the `-std=c2x` to compile for the upcoming C23 standard.

PART II

The C Standard Library

CHAPTER 32

Introduction to C Standard Library

The C compiler is accompanied by a number of useful functions and macros called *the C standard library*. These functions are defined in standard-library header files. To use the C standard-library functions, we simply include the appropriate header into our program. Here are some of the C standard-library headers:

Available in all C standards:

`<assert.h>`	Assertion macros
`<ctype.h>`	Utils for individual characters
`<errno.h>`	Macros reporting error conditions
`<float.h>`	Floating-type limits
`<limits.h>`	Sizes of basic types
`<locale.h>`	Localization utils
`<math.h>`	Math functions
`<setjmp.h>`	Jumps
`<signal.h>`	Signal functions
`<stdarg.h>`	Variable arguments
`<stddef.h>`	Common macros
`<stdio.h>`	Input and output functions
`<stdlib.h>`	General utilities for memory, string, and program flow
`<string.h>`	String manipulation functions

(*continued*)

© Slobodan Dmitrović 2024
S. Dmitrović, *Modern C for Absolute Beginners*, https://doi.org/10.1007/979-8-8688-0224-9_32

`<time.h>`	Time and date
`<wchar.h>`	Multibyte and wide characters utilities
`<wctype.h>`	Wide character types
`<iso646.h>`	Macros for alternative operator spellings

Available since C99:

`<complex.h>`	Complex number arithmetic
`<fenv.h>`	Floating-point environment
`<inttypes.h>`	Format conversion of integer types
`<stdbool.h>`	Type bool
`<stdint.h>`	Fixed-width integer types
`<tgmath.h>`	Generic math and complex macros

Available since C11:

`<threads.h>`	Thread library
`<stdalign.h>`	`alignas` and `alignof` macros
`<stdatomic.h>`	Atomic types
`<stdnoreturn.h>`	noreturn macros
`<uchar.h>`	UTF-16 and UTF-32 utils

Available since C23:

`<stdbit.h>`	Bit and byte utilities
`<stdckdint.h>`	Checked integer arithmetic

The following sections describe some of the most used functions inside the library.

32.1 String Manipulation

Here, we describe a couple of useful functions we use to manipulate our character arrays (strings).

32.1.1 strlen

The strlen function returns the number of characters inside a null-terminated character array, excluding the null-terminating character. The function is of the following signature:

```
sizet_t strlen (const char* str);
```

To use this function, we include the <string.h> header and supply a character array as an argument. Example:

```
#include <stdio.h>
#include <string.h>

int main(void)
{
    const char str[] = "How many characters here?";
    size_t myStrLength = strlen(str);
    printf("The string contains %zu characters.\n", myStrLength);
}
```

Output:

```
The string contains 25 characters.
```

We could rewrite the preceding example to use a const char *p pointer to a character string:

```
#include <stdio.h>
#include <string.h>

int main(void)
{
    const char *p = "How many characters here?";
```

```
        size_t myStrLength = strlen(p);
        printf("The string contains %zu characters.\n", myStrLength);
}
```

Output:

```
The string contains 25 characters.
```

32.1.2 strcmp

The strcmp function compares two strings. If strings are equal, the function returns the value of 0. If strings are not equal, the function returns a value of either < 0 or > 0. The function compares strings one character at a time. When a character from the left-hand string does not match the character from the right-hand-side string, the function can either:

- Return a value less than 0 if the unmatched left-hand side character comes before the right-hand side character in lexicographical order

- Return a value greater than 0 if the unmatched left-hand side character comes after the right-hand side character in lexicographical order

For the most part, we will be checking if two strings are equal. Example:

```
#include <stdio.h>
#include <string.h>

int main(void)
{
        const char *str1 = "Hello World!";
        const char *str2 = "Hello World!";
        if (strcmp(str1, str2) == 0)
        {
                printf("The strings are equal.\n");
        }
        else
        {
                printf("The strings are not equal.\n");
        }
}
```

Output:

```
The strings are equal.
```

32.1.3 strcat

The strcat function concatenates two strings. It appends the source string to the destination string. The function is of the following signature:

```
char *strcat(char *destination, const char *source);
```

To concatenate two strings, we write:

```
#include <stdio.h>
#include <string.h>

int main(void)
{
    char destination_str[30] = "Hello ";
    char source_str[30] = "World!";
    strcat(destination_str, source_str);
    printf("The concatenated string is: %s\n", destination_str);
}
```

Output:

```
The concatenated string is: Hello World!
```

The destination string array must be large enough to accept the concatenated string.

32.1.4 strcpy

The strcpy function copies one string to another. It copies the characters from the source_str string to the destination_str string. The function signature is:

```
char *strcpy(char *destination, const char *source);
```

To copy one string to another, we write:

```
#include <stdio.h>
#include <string.h>

int main(void)
{
    char destination_str[30];
    char source_str[30] = "Hello World!";
    strcpy(destination_str, source_str);
    printf("The copied string is: %s\n", destination_str);
}
```

Output:

```
The copied string is: Hello World!
```

The destination array must be large enough to accommodate the copied characters, including the (invisible) null-terminating character.

32.1.5 strstr

The strstr function searches for a substring inside a string. It returns the first position at which the substring is found. The function is of the following signature:

```
char *strstr(const char* string, const char* substring);
```

To search for a substring within a string, we write:

```
#include <stdio.h>
#include <string.h>

int main(void)
{
    char myString[] = "Hello World!";
    char mySubstring[] = "World";
    if (strstr(myString, mySubstring))
    {
        printf("Substring found.\n");
```

```
        }
        else
        {
                printf("Substring not found.\n");
        }
}
```

Output:

```
Substring found.
```

To print out the position at which the substring was found, we subtract the original string's address from the strstr's function return value as in posFound - myString. Remember, array names get converted to pointers when used as function arguments. Subtracting pointers gives us the position of a substring:

```
#include <stdio.h>
#include <string.h>

int main(void)
{
        char myString[] = "Hello World!";
        char mySubstring[] = "World";
        char *posFound = strstr(myString, mySubstring);
        if (posFound)
        {
                printf("Substring found at position: %ld.\n", posFound - myString);
        }
        else
        {
                printf("Substring not found.\n");
        }
}
```

Output:

```
Substring found at position: 6.
```

32.2 Memory Manipulation Functions

The C standard library provides several functions that allow us to work with bytes inside memory blocks. For example, these functions allow us to set the values of the entire memory block, copy bytes from one memory block to another, compare memory blocks, and more. Note that type `unsigned char` can be used to represent a single byte.

32.2.1 memset

The memory obtained through `malloc` is not initialized. The allocated memory blocks hold no meaningful values. Trying to read uninitialized memory will result in *undefined behavior*. Earlier, we used the `calloc` function to allocate and initialize the memory blocks to zero.

Another way to initialize the memory is through a `memset` function declared inside the `<string.h>` header file. The function has the following signature:

```
void *memset(void *destination, int value, size_t N);
```

The function accepts a pointer to allocated memory here, called `destination`, the `value` to fill the allocated bytes, and the memory block's size in bytes, here named `N`.

To allocate space for five integers and then fill the entire memory block/all the bytes in the allocated memory with zeros, we write:

```
#include <stdio.h>
#include <stdlib.h>
#include <string.h>

int main(void)
{
    int *p = malloc(5 * sizeof(int));
    if (p)
    {
        memset(p, 0, 5 * sizeof(int));
        for (int i = 0; i < 5; i++)
        {
            printf("%d ", p[i]);
```

```
        }
    }
    free(p);
}
```

Output:

---

0 0 0 0 0

32.2.2 memcpy

The memcpy function copies N bytes/characters from a memory location/block pointed to by source to a memory area pointed to by destination. The function is of the following signature:

```
void* memcpy( void *dest, const void *source, size_t N );
```

The function interprets memory bytes as unsigned char. The function is defined inside the <string.h> header. For example, to copy 5 bytes from one string array to another string array, we write:

```
#include <stdio.h>
#include <string.h>

int main(void)
{
    char source[] = "Hello World.";
    char destination[5];
    memcpy(destination, source, sizeof destination);
    printf("The source is: %s\n", source);
    printf("The destination after copying 5 characters is:\n");
    // write a character, one by one, using the putchar() function
    for (size_t i = 0; i < sizeof destination; i++)
    {
        putchar(destination[i]);
    }
}
```

Output:

```
The source is: Hello World.
The destination after copying 5 characters is:
Hello
```

This example copies five characters from a source array to a destination array and uses the putchar() function to print out the destination characters one by one.

To copy an array of elements into a dynamically allocated memory block, we write:

```c
#include <stdio.h>
#include <stdlib.h>
#include <string.h>

int main(void)
{
    int myArr[] = {10, 20, 30, 40, 50};
    // allocate space for 5 integers
    int *p = malloc(5 * sizeof(int));
    // copy bytes from an array to an allocated space
    memcpy(p, myArr, 5 * sizeof(int));
    printf("Copied bytes from an array to an allocated space. The values
    are:\n");
    for (int i = 0; i < 5; i++)
    {
        printf("%d ", p[i]);
    }
    free(p);
}
```

Output:

```
Copied bytes from an array to an allocated space. The values are:
10 20 30 40 50
```

To copy a struct data object into another struct object, we write:

```
#include <stdio.h>
#include <string.h>

typedef struct
{
    char c;
    int x;
    double d;
} MyStruct;

int main(void)
{
    MyStruct source, destination;
    source.c = 'a';
    source.x = 123;
    source.d = 456.789;
    memcpy(&destination, &source, sizeof(destination));
    printf("The result after copying bytes from source to
    destination:\n");
    printf("Member destination.c has a value of: %c\n", destination.c);
    printf("Member destination.x has a value of: %d\n", destination.x);
    printf("Member destination.d has a value of: %f\n", destination.d);
}
```

Output:

```
The result after copying bytes from source to destination:
Member destination.c has a value of: a
Member destination.x has a value of: 123
Member destination.d has a value of: 456.789000
```

Here, we declared two variables of type MyStruct, called source and destination. We populate the data of the source struct and then copy individual bytes of source into destination using memcpy function. Since the memcpy function accepts pointers, we use our structs' addresses: &destination and &source. Now, both structs have identical data.

32.2.3 memcmp

The memcmp function compares the first N bytes from the memory block pointed by p1 to the first N bytes pointed to by p2. The function returns 0 if the byte values match. The function has the following signature:

```
int memcmp( const void* p1, const void* p2, size_t N );
```

To compare two arrays byte by byte using memcmp, we write:

```
#include <stdio.h>
#include <string.h>

int main(void)
{
    int arr1[] = {10, 20, 30, 40, 50};
    int arr2[] = {10, 20, 20, 40, 50};
    int myResult = memcmp(arr1, arr2, 5 * sizeof(int));
    if (myResult == 0)
    {
        printf("The arrays values match.\n");
    }
    else
    {
        printf("The arrays values do not match.\n");
    }
}
```

Output:

```
The arrays values do not match.
```

This example compares the individual bytes of arr1 and arr2. It compares the first 20 bytes of both arrays. Remember, the size of int is 4, times 5 elements, equals 20 bytes in total, the number calculated using the 5 * sizeof(int) expression. Since the arrays are not equal, the function returns a value other than 0.

If the bytes do not match, the memcmp function can return one of the following:

> **<0** – If the first byte that does not match has a lower value in p1 than in p2
>
> **>0** – If the first byte that does not match has a higher value in p1 than in p2

The memcmp function is a convenient way to compare two data objects in memory, byte by byte.

32.2.4 memchr

The memchr function searches for a particular byte c in the initial N characters within a memory block pointed to by p. The function is declared inside the <string.h> header and is of the following signature:

```
void* memchr( const void* p, int c, size_t N );
```

The function searches for the first occurrence of c, and if the byte/char is found, the function returns a pointer to the location of c. If the byte value is not found, the function returns a NULL. Internally, the c byte is interpreted as unsigned char. The following example searches for a byte with a value of 'W' inside a "Hello World!" character array:

```
#include <stdio.h>
#include <string.h>

int main(void)
{
    char mystr[] = "Hello World!";
    char *pfound = memchr(mystr, 'W', strlen(mystr));
    if (pfound != NULL)
    {
        printf("Character/byte found at: %s\n", pfound);
    }
    else
    {
        printf("Character/byte not found: %s\n", pfound);
    }
}
```

Output:

```
Character/byte found at: World!
```

32.3 Mathematical Functions

The C standard library provides a set of useful mathematical functions. The functions are defined inside different header files. Here, we discuss some of the most widely used ones.

32.3.1 abs

The abs function returns an absolute value of an integer argument. The function is defined inside the <stdlib.h> header. Example:

```
#include <stdlib.h>
#include <stdio.h>

int main(void)
{
    int x = -123;
    int y = 456;
    printf("The absolute value of x is: %d\n", abs(x));
    printf("The absolute value of y is: %d\n", abs(y));
}
```

Output:

```
The absolute value of x is: 123
The absolute value of y is: 456
```

There are also labs and llabs functions that return absolute values of long and long long arguments, respectively.

32.3.2 fabs

The fabs function returns an absolute value of a double argument. The function is defined inside the <math.h> header. Example:

```c
#include <math.h>
#include <stdio.h>

int main(void)
{
    double x = -123.456;
    double y = 789.101;
    printf("The absolute value of x is: %f\n", fabs(x));
    printf("The absolute value of y is: %f\n", fabs(y));
}
```

Output:

```
The absolute value of x is: 123.456000
The absolute value of y is: 789.101000
```

There are also fabsf and fabsl versions that return absolute values of float and long double arguments, respectively.

32.3.3 pow

The pow function returns the value of *base* raised to the power of the *exponent*. The function has the following syntax:

```c
double pow(double base, double exponent);
```

The function is declared inside the `<math.h>` header file. Example:

```
#include <math.h>
#include <stdio.h>

int main(void)
{
    printf("The value of 2 to the power of 10 is: %f\n", pow(2, 10));
    printf("The value of 2 to the power of 20 is: %f\n", pow(2, 20));
}
```

Output:

```
The value of 2 to the power of 10 is: 1024.000000
The value of 2 to the power of 20 is: 1048576.000000
```

There are also powf and powl variants that accept float and long double arguments.

32.3.4 round

The round returns the result of rounding the floating-point argument to the nearest integer, rounding halfway away from 0. The function is declared inside the `<math.h>` header file and has the following syntax:

```
double round(double argument);
```

Example:

```
#include <stdio.h>
#include <math.h>

int main(void)
{
    double d = 1.5;
    printf("The result of rounding the %f is: %f\n", d, round(d));
    d = 1.49;
    printf("The result of rounding the %f is: %f\n", d, round(d));
}
```

Output:

```
The result of rounding the 1.500000 is: 2.000000
The result of rounding the 1.490000 is: 1.000000
```

To run this example on Linux, we also need to link with the math library by supplying the -lm flag to our compilation string.

There are also roundf and roundl versions that accept float and long double arguments.

To have a rounding function that will return an integral type, we use the lround function. Example:

```
#include <stdio.h>
#include <math.h>

int main(void)
{
    double d = 1.5;
    printf("The result of rounding the %f is: %ld\n", d, lround(d));
    d = 1.49;
    printf("The result of rounding the %f is: %ld\n", d, lround(d));
}
```

Output:

```
The result of rounding the 1.500000 is: 2
The result of rounding the 1.490000 is: 1
```

32.3.5 sqrt

The sqrt function returns the square root of an argument. This function is declared inside the <math.h> header and has the following syntax:

```
double sqrt(double argument);
```

Example:

```c
#include <stdio.h>
#include <math.h>

int main(void)
{
    double d = 64.;
    printf("The square root of %f is: %f\n", d, sqrt(d));
    d = 256.00;
    printf("The square root of %f is: %f\n", d, sqrt(d));
}
```

Output:

```
The square root of 64.000000 is: 8.000000
The square root of 256.000000 is: 16.000000
```

We use the sqrtf variant for the type float and sqrtl for the type long double.

32.4 String Conversion Functions

There are functions in the C standard library that allow us to convert a string to a number and vice versa. Here, we discuss the strtol for converting a string to a number and snprintf for converting a number to a string.

32.4.1 strtol

The strtol function allows us to convert a string to a long int number. The function is defined inside the <stdlib.h> header and has the following syntax:

```c
long strtol(const char *restrict str, char **restrict str_end, int base);
```

Note   The `restrict` keyword was introduced in C99. It helps the compiler to optimize the code. It also says no other parameter in the function list will point to this address/object.

The `strtol` function takes as many characters as possible from `str` to form an integer number of base `base`. The base represents the base of the interpreted integer and can have values from 2 to 36.

The function can also set the pointer pointed to by `str_end` to point at the one past the last character interpreted. We can also ignore this pointer by passing it a null pointer. To convert a string to a base 10 integer, where we ignore the `str_end` pointer, we write:

```c
#include <stdio.h>
#include <stdlib.h>

int main(void)
{
    const char * str = "123 to a number.";
    long result = strtol(str, NULL, 10);
    printf("The result is: %ld\n", result);
}
```

Output:

```
The result is: 123
```

To convert a string to an integer and get the remainder of the string that could not be converted, we write:

```c
#include <stdio.h>
#include <stdlib.h>

int main(void)
{
    const char * str = "123 to a number.";
    char* str_end;
    long result = strtol(str, &str_end, 10);
```

```
    printf("The result is: %ld\n", result);
    printf("The remainder of the string is: %s\n", str_end);
}
```

Output:

```
The result is: 123
The remainder of the string is:  to a number.
```

32.4.2 snprintf

The snprintf function allows us to convert a number to a formatted string. Whereas the printf writes to standard output, the snprintf writes to a character array. The function is declared inside the <stdio.h> header and has the following syntax:

```
int snprintf(char *restrict str_buffer, size_t buffer_size,
            const char *restrict format, ... );
```

The function writes the result into a string buffer pointed to by str_buffer. The buffer_size is the maximum number of characters to be written. The function writes at most buffer-size - 1 characters, plus the automatically added null-terminating character. To convert a single integer x to a string buffer pointed to by strbuffer, without checking for the return value, we write:

```
#include <stdio.h>
#include <stdlib.h>

int main(void)
{
    int x = 123;
    char strbuffer [100];
    snprintf(strbuffer, sizeof strbuffer, "%d", x);
    printf("The result is: %s\n", strbuffer);
}
```

Output:

```
The result is: 123
```

If successful, the snprintf function returns a number of characters written minus the null terminator. If the conversion is unsuccessful, the function returns a negative number. To convert a single integer to a string and check how many characters were written, we use:

```c
#include <stdio.h>
#include <stdlib.h>

int main(void)
{
    int x = 123;
    char strbuffer [100];
    int nc = snprintf(strbuffer, sizeof strbuffer, "%d", x);
    printf("The result is: %s\n", strbuffer);
    printf("The number of characters written is: %d\n", nc);
}
```

Output:

```
The result is: 123
The number of characters written is: 3
```

To form a more descriptive string out of int and double values, we use the string constant with format specifiers. We also pass in the comma-separated list of numbers. Example:

```c
#include <stdio.h>
#include <stdlib.h>

int main(void)
{
    int x = 123;
    double d = 456.789;
```

```
        char strbuffer[100];
        int nc = snprintf(strbuffer, sizeof strbuffer, "int: %d,
        double: %g", x, d);
        printf("%s\n", strbuffer);
        printf("The number of characters written is: %d\n", nc);
}
```

Output:

```
int: 123, double: 456.789
The number of characters written is: 25
```

PART III

Modern C Standards

CHAPTER 33

Introduction to C11 Standard

The C11 standard, formally known as `ISO/IEC 9899:2011`, was a C standard adopted in late 2011. The C11 standard replaced the C99 standard and was superseded by C17. C11 introduces new features to the C language and C standard library and modifies a few existing ones. Here, we discuss some of the notable features.

33.1 _Static_assert

The `_Static_assert` performs assertion during compile time before our program starts. The static assertion has the following syntax:

```
_Static_assert(expression, message);
```

The static assertion evaluates the constant *expression* during compile time. If the expression is evaluated to 0(`false`), a *message* is displayed, and the compilation fails. If the expression does not evaluate to 0, no message is displayed, and nothing happens. For example, let us check if the size of type `int` is equal to 8 using static assertion. Chances are the size of our `int` is equal to 4 and the assertion will fail. Example:

```
int main(void)
{
    _Static_assert(sizeof(int) == 8, "The size of int is not 8.\n");
}
```

© Slobodan Dmitrović 2024
S. Dmitrović, *Modern C for Absolute Beginners*, https://doi.org/10.1007/979-8-8688-0224-9_33

If we used long instead of int, chances are there will be no error message and the compilation will continue. Example:

```
int main(void)
{
    _Static_assert(sizeof(long) == 8, "The size of long is not 8.\n");
}
```

The _Static_assert keyword can be replaced by a static_assert macro declared inside the <assert.h> header. Example:

```
#include <assert.h>
int main(void)
{
    static_assert(sizeof(int) == 8, "The size of int is not 8.\n");
}
```

In short, static assertions are a convenient way to enforce assertions and catch errors during compile time.

33.2 The _Noreturn Function Specifier

The _Noreturn function specifier, when applied to a function declaration, specifies that the function *does not return*. More precisely, it specifies that the function does not return by

- Executing a return statement

- Hitting the end of the function block marked by the closing brace (})

Having the _Noreturn specifier suppresses some of the spurious warnings and further optimizes the code. Example:

```
#include <stdlib.h>
#include <stdio.h>

_Noreturn void justExit()
{
    printf("This function does not return. Exiting...\n");
    exit(0);
}
```

```
int main(void)
{
    justExit();
}
```

The specifier can be replaced by the equivalent noreturn macro declared inside the <stdnoreturn.h> header. Example:

```
#include <stdlib.h>
#include <stdio.h>
#include <stdnoreturn.h>

noreturn void justExit()
{
    printf("This function does not return. Exiting...\n");
    exit(0);
}

int main(void)
{
    justExit();
}
```

33.3 Type Generic Macros Using _Generic

The use of _Generic provides a way to select one of several expressions during compile time, based on a type of a given controlling expression. The blueprint for a generic expression/macro is:

```
_Generic ( controlling_expression, list_of_associations)
```

The *controlling expression* is an expression whose type will be compared to types listed in the association list. The association list is a comma-separated list of the following content:

```
        type1 : expression1,

        type2 : expression2,

        default : default_expression
```

The type of the controlling expression is compared to the types in the list. If it matches one of them, the generic selection becomes the expression after the colon.

Let us assume we had several functions that accept different types of parameters. We then want to choose the appropriate function based on a type of argument while using a single generic macro name. In that case, we utilize the _Generic selection in the following way:

```c
#include <stdio.h>
#define myfn(X) _Generic((X), \
                                     int : myfn_i, \
                                     float : myfn_f, \
                                     double : myfn_d, \
                                     default : myfn_ld \
                                     )(X)
void myfn_i(int x)
{
    printf("Printing int: %d\n", x);
}

void myfn_f(float x)
{
    printf("Printing float: %f\n", x);
}

void myfn_d(double x)
{
    printf("Printing double: %f\n", x);
}

void myfn_ld(long double x)
{
    printf("Printing long double: %Lf\n", x);
}
```

```
int main(void)
{
    int x = 123;
    float f = 456.789f;
    double d = 101.112;
    long double ld = 134.456l;
    myfn(x);
    myfn(f);
    myfn(d);
    myfn(ld);
}
```

Output:

```
Printing int: 123
Printing float: 456.789001
Printing double: 101.112000
Printing long double: 134.456000
```

This example expands the myfn macro to the appropriate expression based on the type of X. If no type can be matched in the association list, the macro expands to the default expression. The default expression, in our case, is the myfn_ld function. This approach closely matches the *function overloading* concept found in other languages.

33.4 The _Alignof Operator

The _Alignof operator returns the *alignment requirements* of the type. Let us assume we have two data objects in memory of the same type, positioned in successive memory addresses. The alignment requirement is the property of an object that says how many bytes there must be between these two addresses in order to store the objects successfully. The _Alignof operator gets this number for us and has the following blueprint:

```
_Alignof(type_name)
```

Example:

```
#include <stdio.h>

struct S1
{
    char c;
    char d;
};

struct S2
{
    char c;
    int x;
};

int main(void)
{
    printf("The alignment of char: %zu\n", _Alignof(char));
    printf("The alignment of int: %zu\n", _Alignof(int));
    printf("The alignment of struct S1: %zu\n", _Alignof(struct S1));
    printf("The alignment of struct S2: %zu\n", _Alignof(struct S2));
}
```

   Output:

```
The alignment of char: 1
The alignment of int: 4
The alignment of struct S1: 1
The alignment of struct S2: 4
```

There is also a convenience macro called `alignof` inside the `<stdalign.h>` header that expands to our `_Alignof` operator.

33.5 The _Alignas Specifier

The _Alignas specifier modifies the alignment requirement when declaring an object. The _Alignas specifier has two syntaxes, one in which it accepts an *expression* that evaluates to the number of bytes and one in which it accepts a *type name*:

> _Alignas (constant_int_expression)
>
> _Alignas (type_name)

The alignment expression must be a positive power of 2. For example, if we want to enforce a specific alignment of our structure, we write:

```c
#include <stdio.h>

struct MyStruct
{
  _Alignas(16) int x[4];
};

int main(void)
{
    printf("The alignment of MyStruct is: %zu bytes\n", _Alignof(struct
    MyStruct));
}
```

Output:

```
The alignment of MyStruct is: 16 bytes
```

In this example, every object of type `struct MyStruct` will be aligned to a 16-byte boundary. We can also use the `alignas` macro defined inside the `<stdalign.h>` header. The compiler will issue an error if

- The value is not 0 or a positive power of 2

- The value exceeds the maximum allowed alignment

- The value is less than the physically possible minimum alignment

33.6 Anonymous Structures and Unions

Structures (or unions) without a name are called *anonymous structures*. They come in handy when we want to nest a structure (or a union) inside another structure (or a union). Example:

```
#include <stdio.h>

struct MyStruct
{
    int a;
    struct // anonymous structure
    {
        int b;
        int c;
    };
};

int main(void)
{
    struct MyStruct s;
    s.a = 123;
    s.b = 456;
    s.c = 789;
    printf("Field a: %d\n", s.a);
    printf("Inner field b: %d\n", s.b);
    printf("Inner field c: %d\n", s.c);
}
```

   Output:

```
Field a: 123
Inner field b: 456
Inner field c: 789
```

In this example, we used a structure and called it MyStruct. Inside that structure, there is one integer field called a and a nested, anonymous structure having two fields, b and c. To access these fields, we simply use the s.b and s.c syntax as anonymous struct members are members of the enclosing struct.

33.7 Aligned Memory Allocation: aligned_alloc

The C11 standard introduces an aligned_alloc function, which allocates a memory block with a specified alignment. The syntax is:

```
void *aligned_alloc(size_t alignment, size_t size);
```

The function is defined inside the <stdlib.h> header. The memory is not initialized and must be freed with free or deallocated with realloc. The size in bytes must be a multiple of alignment. Example:

```
#include <stdio.h>
#include <stdlib.h>

int main(void)
{
    int *p = aligned_alloc(512, 512 * sizeof *p);
    printf("Allocated a 512-byte aligned memory block.\n");
    printf("The address is: %p\n", (void *)p);
    free(p);
}
```

Output:

```
Allocated a 512-byte aligned memory block.
The address is: 0x55ca95945200
```

33.8 Unicode Support for UTF-16 and UTF-32

The C11 standard provides types for storing UTF-16 and UTF-32 encoded strings. They are char16_t and char32_t. Both types and the Unicode conversion functions are declared in a <uchar.h> header file. Example:

```
#include <uchar.h>

int main(void)
{
    char16_t arr16[] = u"Our 16-bit wide characters here.\n";
    char32_t arr32[] = U"Our 32-bit wide characters here.\n";
}
```

We use the **u** prefix for the char16_t character array and the **U** prefix for the char32_t character array.

The width of the type char16_t can be larger than 16 bits, but the size of the value stored will be exactly 16 bits wide. Similarly, for a char32_t type, the size of the char32_t type itself can be larger than 32 bits, but the value stored inside this type will be exactly 32 bits wide.

33.9 Bounds Checking and Threads Overview

While the detailed analysis of the following features is out of scope for this book, we will briefly mention two additional things introduced in the C11 standard. They are *bounds-checking (safe) functions* and a *thread support library*.

33.9.1 Bounds-Checking Functions

A few string and I/O functions can cause a *buffer overflow*. The C11 standard offers an optional extension containing the so-called *bounds-checking functions* that rectify this problem. These functions are also referred to as safety functions and carry the _s suffix. Some of them are gets_s, fopen_s, printf_s, scanf_s, strcpy_s, and wcscpy_s. The compiler might not provide these, and they are only available if the __STD_LIB_EXT1__ macro is defined.

33.9.2 Threads Support

The C11 standard offers an optional thread support library. The functions are defined inside the <threads.h> header. These functions bring the native thread support to the C language. They allow for creating and joining threads, creating mutexes, synchronizing access, working with conditional variables, and more.

The following example creates a thread that executes a code from a function which accepts one argument:

```c
#include <threads.h>
#include <stdio.h>

int dowork(void *arg)
{
    thrd_t mythreadid = thrd_current();
    for (int i = 0; i < 5; i++)
    {
        printf("Thread id: %lu, counter: %d, code: %s\n", mythreadid,
        i, (char *)arg);
    }
    return 0;
}

int main(void)
{
    thrd_t mythread;
    // create a thread that executes a function code
    if (thrd_success != thrd_create(&mythread, dowork, "Hello from a
    thread!"))
    {
        printf("Could not create a thread.\n");
        return 1;
    }
    // join a thread to the main thread
    thrd_join(mythread, NULL);
}
```

Output:

```
Thread id: 140647017862912, counter: 0, code: Hello from a thread!
Thread id: 140647017862912, counter: 1, code: Hello from a thread!
Thread id: 140647017862912, counter: 2, code: Hello from a thread!
Thread id: 140647017862912, counter: 3, code: Hello from a thread!
Thread id: 140647017862912, counter: 4, code: Hello from a thread!
```

This example defines a function that will be executed by our thread. In the main program, we create/spawn the thread by calling the thrd_create function, to which we pass the address of our local mythread variable, the name of the function to be executed, dowork, and a string representing the function argument. Inside the user-defined function dowork, we also print out the current thread ID obtained through a thrd_current() function call.

When compiling a multithreaded application on Linux, we need to add the -pthread flag to the compilation string:

```
gcc -Wall source.c -std=c11 -pedantic -pthread
```

Note that <threads.h> support is optional and might not be fully implemented in GCC.

CHAPTER 34

The C17 Standard

At the time of writing, the C17 standard, officially named ISO/IEC 9899:2018, is the last published C standard. It replaces the C11 standard, does not introduce new features, and fixes defects reported for C11. The __STDC_VERSION__ macro for this standard has the value of 201710L. To compile for a C17 standard, we include the -stdc=17 flag. Example:

```
gcc -Wall source.c -std=c17 -pedantic
```

The C17 standard is sometimes also referred to as the *C18 standard*. The C17 standard will be replaced by the upcoming standard, informally referred to as the C2X (C23) standard.

© Slobodan Dmitrović 2024
S. Dmitrović, *Modern C for Absolute Beginners*, https://doi.org/10.1007/979-8-8688-0224-9_34

CHAPTER 35

The Upcoming C23 Standard

At the time of writing, there is a new C standard in the making, informally referred to as the C23 or C2X. The standard will probably be published in 2024, with a working draft now available. Currently, we can install gcc version 13 or higher to try out some of the C23 features. We need to include the -std=c2x flag in the compilation string when targeting the C23 standard.

35.1 constexpr

Starting with C23, objects marked with constexpr are constants whose value is determined during the compilation time. The constexpr object must be fully initialized at the point of declaration. Although constexpr objects occupy memory and have an address, they are read-only. The following example uses the constexpr storage specifier applied to several different objects:

```c
#include <stdio.h>

int main(void)
{
    constexpr int x = 123;
    constexpr unsigned u = 456u;
    constexpr char mystring[] = {"Hello."};
    printf("The value of x is: %d\n", x);
    printf("The value of u is: %u\n", u);
    printf("The value of mystring is: %s\n", mystring);
}
```

© Slobodan Dmitrović 2024
S. Dmitrović, *Modern C for Absolute Beginners*, https://doi.org/10.1007/979-8-8688-0224-9_35

Output:

```
The value of x is: 123
The value of u is: 456
The value of mystring is: Hello.
```

The constexpr object can also be used as an initializer in other constant expressions.
Example:

```
#include <stdio.h>

int main(void)
{
    constexpr int x = 10;

    enum
    {
        FIRST = x,
        SECOND,
        THIRD
    };

    constexpr int y = x;
    static int myvar = x + 20;

    int myarray[x]; // valid, not a variable length array

    printf("The value of x is: %d\n.", x);
    printf("The value of y is: %d\n.", y);
    printf("The value of myvar is: %d\n.", myvar);
    printf("Declared an array of %d elements. Valid, not a VLA.\n", x);
}
```

Output:

```
The value of x is: 10
The value of y is: 10
The value of myvar is: 30
Declared an array of 10 elements. Valid, not a VLA.
```

This example uses the constexpr object to initialize an enumerator, another constexpr object, a static variable, and inside an array declaration. Unlike regular constants whose value is determined during runtime, the constexpr object's value is determined during compilation time, and they can safely be used to declare the size of the array without participating in the creation of the variable length array.

35.2 Binary Integer Constants

The C23 standard introduces binary integer constants. The binary constant starts with the 0b or 0B sequence, followed by binary digits 1 and/or 0. This allows us to write down the value of an integer variable using the binary representation. Example:

```
#include <stdio.h>

int main(void)
{
    int x = 0b1010;
    printf("The value of the integer variable x is: %d\n", x);
}
```

Output:

```
The value of the integer variable x is 10
```

The 0b1010 integer constant is a binary representation of a decimal number 10. As with previous standards, we can also add integer suffixes to our binary constant if needed. Let us rewrite the preceding example to use the unsigned type instead:

```
#include <stdio.h>

int main(void)
{
    unsigned x = 0b1010u;
    printf("The value of the unsigned variable x is: %u\n", x);
}
```

Output:

```
The value of the unsigned variable x is: 10
```

We have added the u suffix to our integer constant to avoid implicit conversion from int to unsigned.

Let us now write an example that uses decimal, hexadecimal, octal, and binary integer constants to represent the same value of 100:

```
#include <stdio.h>

int main(void)
{
    int x1 = 100; // decimal
    int x2 = 0x64; // hexadecimal
    int x3 = 0144; // decimal
    int x4 = 0b01100100; // binary

    printf("The value of the variable x1 is: %d\n", x1);
    printf("The value of the variable x2 is: %d\n", x2);
    printf("The value of the variable x3 is: %d\n", x3);
    printf("The value of the variable x4 is: %d\n", x4);
}
```

Output:

```
The value of the variable x1 is: 100
The value of the variable x2 is: 100
The value of the variable x3 is: 100
The value of the variable x4 is: 100
```

35.3 true and false

Starting with C23, we do not have to include any particular header to define bool variables to which we can assign true or false values. These predefined true and false constants are now keywords in C23. Example:

```
#include <stdio.h>

int main(void)
{
    bool condition = true;
    if (condition)
    {
        printf("The condition is true.\n");
    }
    else
    {
        printf("The condition is false.\n");
    }
}
```

Output:

```
The condition is true
```

Prior to C23, we had to include the <stdbool.h> header file to be able to use the bool type.

35.4 nullptr

C23 introduces a new keyword, nullptr, representing a *null pointer constant*. This value is a predefined constant of the underlying nullptr_t type. The type is defined inside a <stddef.h> header file. Prior to C23, we had to use NULL, (void*), or 0 to set the pointer to null pointer constant.

Depending on the implementation, this could potentially cause problems as NULL is a macro. Starting with C23, we can initialize our pointers to a null pointer constant using the keyword nullptr. Example:

```
#include <stdio.h>
#include <stddef.h>

int main(void)
{
    int *p1 = nullptr;
    double *p2 = nullptr;
    struct MyStruct *p3 = nullptr;

printf("The value of the p1 pointer is: %p.\n", (void*)p1);
    printf("The value of the p2 pointer is: %p.\n", (void*)p2);
    printf("The value of the p3 pointer is: %p.\n", (void*)p3);
}
```

Output:

```
The value of the p1 pointer is: (nil).
The value of the p2 pointer is: (nil).
The value of the p3 pointer is: (nil).
```

35.5 Empty initializer ={}

We can utilize an empty initializer in C23 for variables, arrays, and structs using the ={} syntax instead of a ={0} one. When we explicitly initialize an object using the empty initializer, the underlying values are zeroed, and we do not have to use the memset function. Example:

```
#include <stdio.h>

int main(void)
{
    int x = {};

    struct MyStruct
    {
        int a;
        double b;
    } s = {};
```

```
    int arr[5] = {};

    printf("The value of x is: %d.\n", x);
    printf("The value of s.a is: %d.\n", s.a);
    printf("The value of s.b is: %f.\n", s.b);

    printf("The array values are: ");
    for (int i = 0; i < 5; i++)
    {
        printf("%d ", arr[i]);
    }
}
```

Output:

```
The value of x is: 0.
The value of s.a is: 0.
The value of s.b is: 0.000000.
The array values are: 0 0 0 0 0
```

35.6 #embed

The #embed preprocessor directive is used to include the binary resource in our program/build.

To initialize a single variable with the content of some external *somefile.dat* file, using the #embed directive, we write:

```
int main(void)
{
    int x = {
#embed "somefile.dat"
    };
}
```

The preceding example is valid only if *somefile.dat* produces only one value.

To initialize a structure using *somefile.dat*, we write:

```
#include <stdio.h>

int main(void)
{
    struct MyStruct
    {
        int x;
        double d;
    };

    struct MyStruct s = {
    // initializes each field with
    // comma-delimited integer constant-expressions
#embed "somefile.dat"
    };
}
```

In this example, we used the #embed preprocessor directive to initialize a structure since the directive can produce one of the following:

- Comma-separated list of integer constant expressions
- A single integer constant expression
- Nothing (none of the above)

To initialize a fixed-width `unsigned` integer array with the content of a binary resource, such as an external image, we write:

```
#include <stdint.h>
#include <stdio.h>

int main(void)
{
    const uint8_t arr[] = {
#embed "somefile.jpg"
    };
}
```

To initialize a character array with the content of a textual file, we type:

```
#include <stdint.h>
#include <stdio.h>

int main(void)
{
    const char arr[] = {
#embed "myfile.txt"
    };
}
```

The #embed directive can also have parameters. The first one we will discuss is the if_empty parameter. If a binary resource is empty (e.g., the file is empty), the if_empty content replaces the directive. If the resource is not empty, the content of the if_empty token is ignored. Let us modify the previous example to check if the file is empty, and if so, put some content into our char array using the if_empty parameter. Example:

```
#include <stdio.h>

int main(void)
{
    const char arr[] = {
#embed "myfile.txt" if_empty('N', 'o ', ' ', 'd', 'a', 't', 'a')
        , '\0'};
}
```

In this example, we also added the value of '\0', which is a null-terminating character.

In a scenario where we want to initialize a single variable, the if_empty token can simply contain zero:

```
#include <stdio.h>

int main(void)
{
    int x = {
#embed "somefile.dat" if_empty(0)
    };
}
```

If we only want to embed a portion of the resource, we can limit the number of read resource elements (not bytes, but resource elements). An example where we want to embed only the first ten elements from an external resource:

```
#include <stdio.h>

int main(void)
{
    const char arr[] = {
#embed "myfile.txt" limit(10)
    };
}
```

Now, our array should have only ten elements.

35.7 Attributes

There have been many implementation-defined language extensions throughout the years. The adoption of attributes in C23 is an attempt to present a uniform, standard syntax for specifying these extensions/attributes. Attributes are mainly used in declarations and definitions and can relate to types, variables, declarations, and code. The attributes syntax is:

```
[[attribute-list]] what_the_attribute_relates_to
```

One of the attributes can be [[deprecated]]. It marks the declaration as deprecated/obsolete, causing the compiler to issue a warning. Example:

```
#include <stdio.h>

// deprecated definition
[[deprecated]]
void myoldfunction()
{
    printf("This is a deprecated function.\n");
}
```

```
int main(void)
{
    myoldfunction();
    printf("Using deprecated code.\n");
}
```

Some of the other attributes are

- [[fallthrough]] – Where the fallthrough from the previous case is indeed expected

- [[maybe_unused]] – When we want to suppress compiler warnings on unused names

- [[nodiscard]] – Where we expect the compiler to issue a warning when the return value is discarded

35.8 No Parameters Function Declaration

We can now declare a function that accepts no parameters without the need for the inclusion of a void text inside parentheses. We can now ensure the function's behavior will be as intended. Example:

```
#include <stdio.h>

void noparamsfn()
{
    printf("This function does not accept parameters.\n");
}

int main(void)
{
    noparamsfn();
}
```

Output:

```
This function does not accept parameters.
```

35.9 The strdup Function

The strdup function returns a pointer to a copy of a string. It does so as if the place for a copy was allocated using malloc. The function is declared inside the <string.h> header and has the following syntax:

```
char *strdup(const char* arg);
```

The pointer obtained through strdup must be freed afterward. Example:

```
#include <string.h>
#include <stdlib.h>
#include <stdio.h>

int main(void)
{
    const char *s1 = "This will be duplicated.";
    char *s2 = strdup(s1);
    printf("The result is: %s\n", s2);
    free(s2);
}
```

Output:

```
The result is: This will be duplicated.
```

There is also a strndup variant that copies N bytes from the source string and has the following syntax:

```
char *strndup(const char* arg, size_t N);
```

Example:

```
#include <string.h>
#include <stdlib.h>
#include <stdio.h>
```

```
int main(void)
{
    const char *s1 = "This will be duplicated.";
    char *s2 = strndup(s1, 17);
    printf("The result is: %s\n", s2);
    free(s2);
}
```

Output:

```
The result is: This will be dupl
```

35.10 The memccpy Function

The memccpy function copies characters from a data object pointed to by *source* to a memory/object pointed to by *destination*. The function stops copying after any of the two conditions are met:

- N characters were copied.

- The character c is found.

The function is declared inside the <string.h> header and has the following syntax:

```
void *memccpy(void *restrict destination, const void *restrict source,
int c, size_t N);
```

Example:

```
#include <stdio.h>
#include <string.h>

int main(void)
{
    const char source[] = "Copy this until ~ is found.";
    char destination[sizeof source];
    const char stopchar = '~';
```

```
    void *p = memccpy(destination, source, stopchar, sizeof destination);
    if (p)
    {
        printf("Terminating character found. The result is:\n");
        printf("%s\n", destination);
    }
    else
    {
        printf("Terminating character not found. The result is:\n");
        printf("%s\n", destination);
    }
}
```

Output:

```
Terminating character found. The result is:
Copy this until ~
```

If the terminating character stopchar is found, the function returns a pointer to the next character in the destination string after the stopchar. The function returns a null pointer if the terminating character is not found.

PART IV

Dos and Don'ts

CHAPTER 36

Do Not Use the gets Function

The gets function is declared inside the `<stdio.h>` header, reads the input into a character array pointed to by str, and has the following syntax:

```
char *gets (char* str);
```

This function is hazardous as it can cause a buffer overflow and allows for potential buffer overflow attacks. The function is deprecated in the C99 standard and removed in the C11 standard. Do not use this function!

The workaround is to use the fgets alternative. Unlike gets, the fgets function performs bounds checking and is safe from buffer overflow scenarios.

To use the fgets, we simply pass in the pointer to a buffer buff, the maximum number of characters that can be read, and stdio representing our standard input/keyboard. A simple example:

```c
#include <stdio.h>

int main(void)
{
    char buff[100];
    printf("Please enter a string:\n");
    fgets(buff, 100, stdin);
    printf("The result is: %s\n", buff);
}
```

© Slobodan Dmitrović 2024
S. Dmitrović, *Modern C for Absolute Beginners*, https://doi.org/10.1007/979-8-8688-0224-9_36

Output:

```
Please enter a string:
Do not use the gets function!
The result is: Do not use the gets function!
```

Alternatively, opt for a gets_s function, which might be available on our C implementation as part of the optional bounds-checking interfaces extension.

CHAPTER 37

Initialize Variables Before Using Them

When we declare local variables, they are not initialized. Their values are undetermined. Trying to access uninitialized variables causes *undefined behavior*. One use case would be trying to print local, uninitialized variables. The following example demonstrates what should be avoided:

```
#include <stdio.h>

int main(void)
{
    char c;
    int x;
    double d;
    printf("Accessing uninitialized variables...\n");
    printf("%c, %d, %f\n", c, x, d); // undefined behavior
}
```

Possible Output:

```
Accessing uninitialized variables...
[, 32767, 0.000000
```

We are trying to access/print out uninitialized local variables in this example. This leads to undefined behavior and is best avoided.

© Slobodan Dmitrović 2024
S. Dmitrović, *Modern C for Absolute Beginners*, https://doi.org/10.1007/979-8-8688-0224-9_37

We should always initialize (or assign values to) our variables before using them. Example:

```c
#include <stdio.h>

int main(void)
{
    char c = 'a';
    int x = 0;
    double d = 0.0;
    printf("Accessing initialized variables...\n");
    printf("%c, %d, %f\n", c, x, d); // OK
}
```

Output:

```
Accessing initialized variables...
a, 0, 0.000000
```

CHAPTER 38

Do Not Read Out of Bounds

Trying to access an array element that is not there invokes *undefined behavior*. We say we are *reading out of bounds*. The following example demonstrates a common scenario of trying to access a nonexistent, out-of-bounds array element:

```
#include <stdio.h>

int main(void)
{
    int arr[5] = {10, 20, 30, 40, 50};
    printf("Trying to read out of bounds...\n");
    printf("The non-existent array element is: %d\n", arr[5]);
}
```

Possible Output:

```
Trying to read out of bounds...
The non-existent array element is: 32767
```

In this example, we declared an array of five integers. We then try to access a sixth array element using a[5]. But since there is no element a[5], we are invoking undefined behavior. This might cause our program to do anything, including the strange output result earlier. The same effect would be if we tried to access a[10], a[256], etc. We can only access elements a[0] through a[4]. If we want to access only the last array element, we can rewrite the preceding example to be:

© Slobodan Dmitrović 2024
S. Dmitrović, *Modern C for Absolute Beginners*, https://doi.org/10.1007/979-8-8688-0224-9_38

```c
#include <stdio.h>

int main(void)
{
    int arr[5] = {10, 20, 30, 40, 50};
    printf("Accessing the existing array element...\n");
    printf("The existent array element is: %d\n", arr[4]);
}
```

Output:

```
Accessing the existent array element...
The existent array element is: 50
```

CHAPTER 39

Do Not Free the Allocated Memory Twice

Trying to free the allocated memory *two times* causes undefined behavior. The following example shows the wrong usage of two free statements:

```c
#include <stdio.h>
#include <stdlib.h>

int main(void)
{
    printf("Allocating memory...\n");
    int *p = malloc(sizeof(int));
    *p = 123;
    printf("The value is: %d\n", *p);
    printf("Freeing twice - undefined behavior.\n");
    free(p);
    free(p); // undefined behavior
}
```

Possible Output:

```
Allocating memory...
The value is: 123
Freeing twice - undefined behavior.
free(): double free detected in tcache 2
Aborted (core dumped)
```

© Slobodan Dmitrović 2024
S. Dmitrović, *Modern C for Absolute Beginners*, https://doi.org/10.1007/979-8-8688-0224-9_39

In this example, we wrongly tried to free the already freed memory by invoking a second free(p); statement.

The correct way is to free the allocated memory *only once*:

```c
#include <stdio.h>
#include <stdlib.h>

int main(void)
{
    printf("Allocating memory...\n");
    int *p = malloc(sizeof(int));
    *p = 123;
    printf("The value is: %d\n", *p);
    printf("Freeing the memory only once.\n");
    free(p); // OK
}
```

Output:

```
Allocating memory...
The value is: 123
Freeing the memory only once.
```

CHAPTER 40

Do Not Cast the Result of malloc

In C, we do not need to cast the result of malloc. The following example wrongly performs the cast:

```c
#include <stdio.h>
#include <stdlib.h>

int main(void)
{
    printf("Casting the result of malloc. Not needed!\n");
    int *p = (int *)malloc(sizeof(int));
    *p = 123;
    printf("The result is: %d\n", *p);
    free(p);
}
```

Output:

```
Casting the result of malloc. Not needed!
The result is: 123
```

This example casts the result of malloc to type int*. This is unnecessary as the malloc's return value type is void*. And void* is safely and implicitly convertible to the correct pointer type. The cast also adds unneeded code clutter. The proper example would be:

```c
#include <stdio.h>
#include <stdlib.h>

int main(void)
```

© Slobodan Dmitrović 2024
S. Dmitrović, *Modern C for Absolute Beginners*, https://doi.org/10.1007/979-8-8688-0224-9_40

```
{
    printf("Allocating memory without casting.\n");
    int *p = malloc(sizeof(int));
    *p = 123;
    printf("The result is: %d\n", *p);
    free(p);
}
```

Output:

```
Allocating memory without casting.
The result is: 123
```

Furthermore, we could also replace the sizeof(int) expression with the sizeof *p expression to not depend on the type name. Example:

```
#include <stdio.h>
#include <stdlib.h>

int main(void)
{
    printf("Allocating memory without casting.\n");
    int *p = malloc(sizeof *p);
    *p = 123;
    printf("The result is: %d\n", *p);
    free(p);
}
```

Output:

```
Allocating memory without casting.
The result is: 123
```

This casting habit probably stems from the world of C++, where the cast is needed. The rule of thumb is as follows: in C, we do not need to cast the result of malloc, while in C++, we should. We should remember that C and C++ are two different programming languages with different sets of rules.

CHAPTER 41

Do Not Overflow a Signed Integer

There are lower and upper limits to values a signed integer can hold. An INT_MAX macro represents the maximum signed integer value, and the minimum signed integer value is represented by the INT_MIN macro. These macros are declared inside the <limits.h> header.

Trying to store the value that is higher than the allowable maximum or lower than the allowable minimum causes *undefined behavior*. Example:

```c
#include <stdio.h>
#include <limits.h>

int main(void)
{
    int x = INT_MAX;
    printf("The maximum integer value is: %d\n", x);
    printf("Trying to store a value higher than the maximum...\n");
    x = INT_MAX + 1; // undefined behavior
    printf("The variable value is now: %d\n", x);
}
```

Output:

```
The maximum integer value is: 2147483647
Trying to store a value higher than the maximum...
The variable value is now: -2147483648
```

© Slobodan Dmitrović 2024
S. Dmitrović, *Modern C for Absolute Beginners*, https://doi.org/10.1007/979-8-8688-0224-9_41

This example tries to store the number that is higher than the allowable maximum for type int. This causes undefined behavior and the so-called *integer overflow*, resulting in strange negative value output. We should make sure we do not try to store signed integer values outside the allowable range.

Note   Overflowing an **unsigned** integer is well-defined, but it should also be avoided.

CHAPTER 42

Cast a Pointer to void* When Printing Through printf

When printing out a pointer's value (the memory address it points to) using a `printf` function and a `%p` format specifier, we need to cast that pointer to type `void*` first. Simply trying to print out the pointer value through `printf` causes undefined behavior. Example:

```
#include <stdio.h>

int main(void)
{
    int x = 123;
    int *p = &x;
    printf("The pointer value is: %p\n", p); // undefined behavior
}
```

Possible Output:

```
The pointer value is: 0x7ffc57d762ec
```

This example causes undefined behavior because the `%p` format specifier expects a type `void*`, and we are passing in `int*`. The same applies when trying to print out any other pointer type.

© Slobodan Dmitrović 2024
S. Dmitrović, *Modern C for Absolute Beginners*, https://doi.org/10.1007/979-8-8688-0224-9_42

We need to cast the pointer to type void* when printing out the pointer's value using a printf function and the %p conversion specifier. Example:

```
#include <stdio.h>

int main(void)
{
    int x = 123;
    int *p = &x;
    printf("The pointer value is: %p\n", (void *)p); // OK
}
```

Possible Output:

```
The pointer value is: 0x7ffe9d9262dc
```

CHAPTER 43

Do Not Divide by Zero

Trying to divide by zero (0) causes undefined behavior, as shown in the following example:

```c
#include <stdio.h>

int main(void)
{
    printf("Trying to divide with zero...\n");
    int x = 123;
    int y = x / 0; // undefined behavior
    printf("The result is: %d\n", y);
}
```

Possible Output:

```
Trying to divide with zero...
Floating point exception (core dumped)
```

Similar to math rules, we should not divide by zero in C either. The preceding example causes undefined behavior.

© Slobodan Dmitrović 2024
S. Dmitrović, *Modern C for Absolute Beginners*, https://doi.org/10.1007/979-8-8688-0224-9_43

CHAPTER 44

Where to Use Pointers?

In this chapter, we discuss several pointers use cases, including the use of pointers as function parameters.

44.1 Pointers to Existing Objects

Pointers can point to existing data objects using the address-of operator &. Example:

```c
#include <stdio.h>

int main(void)
{
    char mychar = 'A';
    char *p = &mychar;
    printf("The pointed-to value is: %c\n", *p);
}
```

Output:

```
The pointed-to value is: A
```

This example defines a variable of type char and makes the pointer point at that variable/data object using the & operator. The variable's type char is matched by pointers char * type. If we want a pointer pointing to an existing int object, we will use the int * type for a pointer. Example:

© Slobodan Dmitrović 2024
S. Dmitrović, *Modern C for Absolute Beginners*, https://doi.org/10.1007/979-8-8688-0224-9_44

```
#include <stdio.h>

int main(void)
{
        int myvar = 123;
        int *p = &myvar;
        printf("The pointed-to value is: %d\n", *p);
}
```

Output:

```
The pointed-to value is: 123
```

44.2 Pointers to Arrays

A pointer can point to an array. We can simply assign the *array name* to a *pointer name* without using the & operator. The pointer then points at the first element of the array. Example:

```
#include <stdio.h>

int main(void)
{
        int arr[] = {10, 20, 30, 40, 50};
        int *p = arr;
        printf("The first array element is: %d\n", *p);
}
```

Output:

```
The first array element is: 10
```

To print out the next array element, we can use pointer arithmetics. By adding 1 to our pointer, we increase the address it points to by 1 (1 times the size of the pointed-to element), which is the second array element with a value of 20. Example:

```c
#include <stdio.h>

int main(void)
{
    int arr[] = {10, 20, 30, 40, 50};
    int *p = arr;
    printf("The first array element is: %d\n", *p);
    p++;
    printf("The next array element is: %d\n", *p);
}
```

Output:

```
The first array element is: 10
The next array element is: 20
```

To access all array elements using a pointer, we can dereference a pointer using a subscript operator [ ] in combination with an index/counter to iterate through all array elements:

```c
#include <stdio.h>

int main(void)
{
    int arr[] = {10, 20, 30, 40, 50};
    int *p = arr;
    printf("Printing array elements using a pointer:\n");
    for (int i = 0; i < 5; i++)
    {
        printf("%d ", p[i]);
    }
}
```

Output:

```
Printing array elements using a pointer:
10 20 30 40 50
```

44.3 Pointers to String Constants

A string constant is an array of characters enclosed in double quotes. The following is a string constant:

```
"Hello World!"
```

The string constant is a character array made up of visible characters plus one invisible, null-terminating \0 character at the end. The type of string constant/character array is char[]. We can directly assign this string constant to our pointer of type char*. Example:

```
#include <stdio.h>

int main(void)
{
    char *str = "Hello World!";
    printf("The value is: %s\n", str);
}
```

Output:

```
The value is: Hello World!
```

Since the string constant itself is read-only and cannot be modified, we should also add the const qualifier:

```
#include <stdio.h>
int main(void)
{
    const char *str = "This string can not be modified!";
    printf("The value is: %s\n", str);
}
```

Output:

```
The value is: This string can not be modified!
```

Note   We **do not** free the pointers to existing variables, arrays, and string constants. We only free the pointers to dynamically allocated memory.

We discuss pointers to dynamically allocated memory in the following sections.

44.4 Pointers to Dynamically Allocated Memory

Memory obtained through calls to `malloc`, `calloc`, and `realloc` is *dynamically allocated memory*. Pointers can point to this newly allocated memory (block). The dynamically allocated memory must be explicitly freed when we no longer need it. The following example dynamically allocates a memory block for one integer using `malloc`:

```c
#include <stdio.h>
#include <stdlib.h>

int main(void)
{
    printf("Allocating memory...\n");
    int *p = malloc(sizeof(int)); // allocate the memory
    if (p)
    {
        *p = 123456; // manipulate memory
        printf("The value is: %d\n", *p);
    }
    printf("Deallocating memory...\n");
    free(p); // deallocate the memory
    printf("Done.\n");
}
```

Output:

```
Allocating memory...
The value is: 123456
Deallocating memory...
Done.
```

Note   Dynamically allocated memory obtained through `malloc`, `calloc`, or `realloc` **must be** explicitly freed/deallocated.

44.5 Pointers as Function Arguments

Functions can have parameters of pointer types. We pass pointers to these functions as arguments. The following example defines a function that expects an integer pointer as an argument and modifies the pointed-to value. Example:

```
#include <stdio.h>
#include <stdlib.h>

void myfunction(int *arg)
{
    *arg = 456;
}

int main(void)
{
    int x = 123;
    int *p = &x;
    printf("The pointed-to value before the function call: %d\n", *p);
    myfunction(p);
    printf("The pointed-to value after the function call: %d\n", *p);
}
```

Output:

```
The pointed-to value before the function call: 123
The pointed-to value after the function call: 456
```

This example defines a function that accepts a pointer as an argument. The function then modifies the pointed-to value by dereferencing an argument. In the main function, one pointer p points to an int variable called x. We pass that pointer to our function, and the function modifies the pointed-to value.

To pass a *regular variable* to our function accepting a pointer, we pass in the *address of a variable/object*. Example:

```c
#include <stdio.h>
#include <stdlib.h>

void myfunction(int *arg)
{
      *arg = 456;
}
int main(void)
{
      int x = 123;
      printf("The value before the function call: %d\n", x);
      myfunction(&x); // pass in the address of x
      printf("The value after the function call: %d\n", x);
}
```

Output:

```
The value before the function call: 123
The value after the function call: 456
```

This example uses the address of x (&x) expression as an argument for our function accepting a pointer type. We say we pass the argument *by address/reference*.

Suppose a function needs to modify the pointer's value (not the pointed-to value). For example, the function increments the value of a pointer by one. In that case, we use a double pointer for a function parameter and pass in the address of a pointer variable in the main program. Example:

```c
#include <stdio.h>
#include <stdlib.h>

void myfunction(int **arg)
{
      (*arg)++;
}
```

```
int main(void)
{
    int arr[] = {10, 20, 30};
    int *p = arr;
    printf("Pointer value before the function call: %p\n", (void *)p);
    printf("Pointed-to value before the function call: %d\n", *p);
    myfunction(&p); // pass in the pointer
    printf("Pointer value after the function call: %p\n", (void *)p);
    printf("Pointed-to value after the function call: %d\n", *p);
}
```

Possible Output:

```
Pointer value before the function call: 0x7fffe590b22c
Pointed-to value before the function call: 10
Pointer value after the function call: 0x7fffe590b230
Pointed-to value after the function call: 20
```

The function accepts an argument of type int ** (a pointer to a pointer type). It dereferences the double pointer using the *arg expression (to an actual pointer type, int*) and increments it using the ++ operator. The parentheses inside the (*arg)++ expression ensure the dereferencing occurs before incrementing. The function increments the value of a pointer itself. In the main program, we have a pointer pointing to an array's first element. After the function call, its value is incremented, and the pointer p now points at the second array element.

In combination with structures, pointers can also be used to create in-memory data structures, such as linked lists, binary trees, and similar.

CHAPTER 45

Prefer Functions to Function-Like Macros

We should prefer writing and using *real functions* to *function-like macros*. While it might be tempting to write and use function-like macros instead of functions, this might not be a good choice for the following reasons:

- Macros can cause side effects.

- No type checking is performed.

- Macros are preprocessed, not compiled.

- They do not check compiler errors and are harder to debug.

Consider the following example, which uses a macro-like function to square a given parameter:

```c
#include <stdio.h>

#define SQR(a) ((a) * (a))

int main(void)
{
    int x = 1;
    int result = SQR(++x);
    printf("With the macro: %d\n", result);
}
```

Output:

```
With the macro: 9
```

© Slobodan Dmitrović 2024
S. Dmitrović, *Modern C for Absolute Beginners*, https://doi.org/10.1007/979-8-8688-0224-9_45

This example defines a function-like macro that squares a value. For illustration purposes, we pass in a ++x expression as an argument. We get the value of 9 and not 4 as otherwise expected. This is because the SQR macro expands to ((++a) * (++a)), and the value a gets incremented two times. Value a now becomes 3, and 3 squared is equal to 9.

When using a function, we get the expected result of 4. Example:

```
#include <stdio.h>

#define SQR(a) ((a) * (a))

int sqr(int a)
{
    return a * a;
}

int main(void)
{
    int x = 1;
    int result = SQR(++x);
    printf("With the macro: %d\n", result);
    int y = 1;
    result = sqr(++y);
    printf("With the function: %d\n", result);
}
```

Output:

```
With the macro: 9
With the function: 4
```

CHAPTER 46

static Global Names

When we define a variable or a function inside the file/global scope, they have *external linkage* by default. They can be referred to from other .c files/translation units. The static keyword in front of variables and functions in a global scope marks them visible only to the current source file/translation unit, the unit in which they are declared/ defined. We say the static specifier makes them have *internal linkage.* So, globals we do not want to share with other .c files should be marked as static. Both globals globalx and globalfn() are defined inside the *source.c* file and can be referred to from other *.c* files as well:

```c
#include <stdio.h>

// global scope

int globalx = 123;

void globalfn(void)
{
    printf("The value of a global var is: %d\n", globalx);
}

int main(void)
{
    // local scope
    int localx = 456;
    globalfn();
    printf("The value of a local var is: %d\n", localx);
}
```

© Slobodan Dmitrović 2024
S. Dmitrović, *Modern C for Absolute Beginners*, https://doi.org/10.1007/979-8-8688-0224-9_46

Output:

```
The value of a global var is: 123
The value of a local var is: 456
```

Instead, we can opt for static globals declarations, rendering our `globalx` and `globalfn()` globals visible only to our *source.c* file/translation unit:

```c
#include <stdio.h>

// global scope

static int globalx = 123;

static void globalfn(void)
{
    printf("The value of a global var is: %d\n", globalx);
}

int main(void)
{
    // local scope
    int localx = 456;
    globalfn();
    printf("The value of a local var is: %d\n", localx);
}
```

Output:

```
The value of a global var is: 123
The value of a local var is: 456
```

The `static` specifier is now applied to our globals, making them invisible to other translation units. We say the names now have *internal linkage,* making them visible only to the current translation unit/source file.

CHAPTER 47

What to Put in Header Files?

This chapter explains what to and what not to keep in header files. In general, when we want to share data between multiple source files, we create a common header file and include it in each source file. For the following examples, we will use two source files and one common header file:

- myheaderfile.h – Shared header file

- source.c – Main source file

- source2.c – Second source file

A good practice is to guard the content of the *myheaderfile.h* file with the *include guards/header guards*:

```
#ifndef MYHEADERFILE_H
#define MYHEADERFILE_H
// header source code goes here
#endif
```

47.1 Shared Macros

We can include a macro definition in our header file. This will make it accessible across multiple source files/translation units. The *myheaderfile.h* file:

```
#ifndef MYHEADERFILE_H
#define MYHEADERFILE_H
#define MYMACRO 123
#endif
```

© Slobodan Dmitrović 2024
S. Dmitrović, *Modern C for Absolute Beginners*, https://doi.org/10.1007/979-8-8688-0224-9_47

Then, we include that header file in our *source.c* file:

```
#include "myheaderfile.h"
#include <stdio.h>

void myfunction(); // declaration of a function defined inside a source2.c

int main(void)
{
    printf("Calling macro from a main: %d\n", MYMACRO);
    myfunction();
}
```

And we include the same header file in our *source2.c* file:

```
#include "myheaderfile.h"
#include <stdio.h>

void myfunction(void)
{
    printf("Calling macro from a function inside a source2.c: %d\n",
    MYMACRO);
}
```

We compile both source files using the following syntax:

```
gcc -Wall source.c source2.c -std=c11 -pedantic && ./a.out
```

Output:

```
Calling macro from a main: 123
Calling macro from a function inside a source2.c: 123
```

Summary: We created a common header file and put a macro definition code in that file. We then included the header file in both source files. The MYMACRO is now accessible from both the main (and any other) function inside *source.c* and myfunction (and any other) function inside *source2.c*.

Note how we also needed to create a myfunction declaration inside a *source.c* to be able to call it. The next section explains how to move the function declaration to our header file.

47.2 Function Declarations

When we want to share access to global functions across multiple source files, we put those function declarations inside a common header file. If a function is defined inside a file scope in any source file and we want to use it in other source files, we put that function's declaration inside a shared header file. Example of a *myheaderfile.h* file:

```
#ifndef MYHEADERFILE_H
#define MYHEADERFILE_H

void myfunction(); // function declaration
// this function is defined inside the source2.c file

#endif
```

The *source.c* file content:

```
#include "myheaderfile.h"
#include <stdio.h>

int main(void)
{
    printf("Calling a function defined in the source2.c file:\n");
    myfunction();
}
```

The *source2.c* file:

```
#include "myheaderfile.h"
#include <stdio.h>

// function definition
void myfunction(void)
{
    printf("This function is defined inside the source2.c.\n");
}
```

We compile both source files and observe the following output:

```
Calling a function defined in the source2.c file:
This function is defined inside the source2.c.
```

Summary: In our *myheaderfile.h*, we provided a `myfunction` declaration. Then we included the header file in both source files. The `myfunction` function itself is defined in a global/file scope inside a *source2.c* file. We can now call a `myfunction` function from any source file that includes the *myheaderfile.h* file. We say the function now has *shared access*.

47.3 Shared extern Variables and Constants

With shared global variables or constants, things are more involved than just putting the variable definition inside a shared file. We need to put the shared variables declarations inside the header file and mark them as `extern`. Then, we need to define them only once in some source file.

The `extern` specifier says the name has external linkage and is accessible across multiple source files/translation units. Global names, including functions, are `extern` by default, and we do not need to explicitly use extern on global functions. The `extern` also means the object will have a static storage duration.

While the use of global variables is debatable, this approach allows us to have a centralized place for all our shared constants and variables. The *myheaderfile.h* file is:

```
#ifndef MYHEADERFILE_H
#define MYHEADERFILE_H

// shared constants and variables declarations
extern const int MY_MAX;
extern const char *MY_MESSAGE;
extern const double MY_PI;

// shared variables
extern int mysharedint;
extern double myshareddouble;

#endif
```

The *source.c* file is:

```
#include "myheaderfile.h"
#include <stdio.h>
```

```
// myfunction declaration
void myfunction(void);

int main(void)
{
    printf("Accessing shared constants from source.c:\n");
    printf("%d, %s, %f\n", MY_MAX, MY_MESSAGE, MY_PI);
    printf("Accessing shared global variables from source.c:\n");
    printf("%d %f\n", mysharedint, myshareddouble);
    myfunction(); // defined inside the source2.c file
}
```

And the *source2.c* file is:

```
#include "myheaderfile.h"
#include <stdio.h>

// shared constants definitions
const int MY_MAX = 123;
const char *MY_MESSAGE = "This is a constant string.";
const double MY_PI = 3.14;
// shared variables definitions
int mysharedint = 123;
double myshareddouble = 456.789;
void myfunction(void)
{
    printf("\nAccessing shared constants from source2.c:\n");
    printf("%d, %s, %f\n", MY_MAX, MY_MESSAGE, MY_PI);
    printf("Accessing shared global variables from source2.c:\n");
    printf("%d %f\n", mysharedint, myshareddouble);
}
```

Output:

```
Accessing shared constants from source.c:
123, This is a constant string., 3.140000
Accessing shared global variables from source.c:
123 456.789000
```

```
Accessing shared constants from source2.c:
123, This is a constant string., 3.140000
Accessing shared global variables from source2.c:
123 456.789000
```

With shared global variables and shared constants, things are a bit more involved. First, we need to declare the shared variables and constants in the *myheaderfile.h* file and marked them as extern. Then, we need to define them *only once* inside one of the source files. We can access shared globals from any source file by including the shared myheaderfile.h file in both source files.

The header file should not provide the definition, only the declaration. The source file should not contain external declarations, only definitions.

47.4 Other Header Files

Our header file can also include other header files if needed. For example, our user-defined header file can include both the standard-library and user-defined header files.

The *myheaderfile.h* file that includes other headers can look like:

```
#ifndef MYHEADERFILE_H
#define MYHEADERFILE_H

#include <stdio.h> // include the standard library header
#include "userdefined.h" // include the user-defined header

#endif
```

PART V

Appendices

APPENDIX A

Linkage

When we compile our source code, the compiler stitches a header and the source file's content to create a single source file called a *translation unit*. The translation unit is then used to produce an *object file*. If we compile multiple source files, we get multiple object files. The linker then assembles these object files to produce an *executable file*.

A *linkage* can be seen as a name's property that determines the name's accessibility across translation units. By *name*, we mean *variables and functions*. If a name is visible only to/inside a *current* translation unit, we say it has *internal linkage*. If a name is visible to *all* translation units, we say it has an *external linkage*.

Static global names have internal linkage. Example:

```c
#include <stdio.h>

// global scope
static int x = 123; // internal linkage
static void myfunction() // internal linkage
{
    printf("The value is: %d\n", x);
}

int main(void)
{
    printf("Calling a global function with internal linkage.\n");
    myfunction();
}
```

Output:

```
Calling a global function with internal linkage.
The value is: 123
```

© Slobodan Dmitrović 2024
S. Dmitrović, *Modern C for Absolute Beginners*, https://doi.org/10.1007/979-8-8688-0224-9_48

Names declared inside a global/file scope have *external linkage* by default. Example:

```c
#include <stdio.h>

// global scope
int x = 123; // external linkage
void myfunction() // external linkage
{
     printf("The value is: %d\n", x);
}

int main(void)
{
     printf("Calling a global function with external linkage.\n");
     myfunction();
}
```

Output:

```
Calling a global function with external linkage.
The value is: 123
```

Local names (names local to a function) have no linkage. Example:

```c
#include <stdio.h>

// global scope
int main(void)
{
     // local scope
     int x = 123; // no linkage
     printf("The value of a variable with no linkage is: %d\n", x);
}
```

Output:

```
The value of a variable with no linkage is: 123
```

APPENDIX B

Time and Date

The `<time.h>` header declares functions that allow us to work with date-time. This chapter explains how to obtain and format the current time and date.

The `time` function is declared inside the `<time.h>` header and returns the current date-time (date-time since epoch) as an object of type `time_t`. The function has the following signature:

```
timet_ time(time_t *arg);
```

The type `time_t` is a type capable of storing times. The time function can return the calendar time when `arg` is NULL:

```c
#include <stdio.h>
#include <time.h>

int main(void)
{
    time_t mytime = time(NULL);
    printf("Obtained the current time to a mytime variable.\n");
}
```

Or store it inside an object pointed to by `arg`:

```c
#include <stdio.h>
#include <time.h>

int main(void)
{
    time_t mytime;
    time(&mytime);
    printf("Obtained the current time to a mytime variable.\n");
}
```

© Slobodan Dmitrović 2024
S. Dmitrović, *Modern C for Absolute Beginners*, https://doi.org/10.1007/979-8-8688-0224-9_49

There are several steps involved when getting and formatting the time.

- Get the current date-time using a `time` function.

- Store/convert the obtained date-time into a `tm` struct using `localtime` or `gmtime`.

- Format the obtained time using the `strftime`.

The following example obtains a date-time and stores it into a `tm` struct using a `localtime` function:

```c
#include <stdio.h>
#include <time.h>

int main(void)
{
    time_t mytime = time(NULL);
    struct tm *now;
    now = localtime(&mytime);
    printf("Obtained and stored the current time.\n");
}
```

The `localtime` function converts obtained local time to a `tm` calendar time. The `tm` structure holds the calendar date and time. The `tm` structure has the following predefined member fields of type `int`:

- `tm_sec` – Seconds from 0 to 60

- `tm_min` – Minutes from 0 to 59

- `tm_hour` – Hours from 0 to 23

- `tm_mday` – Days from 1 to 31

- `tm_mon` – Months from 0 to 11

- `tm_year` – Years since 1900

- `tm_wday` – Days since Sunday from 0 to 6

- `tm_yday` – Days since January the 1st from 0 to 365

- `tm_isdst` – Daytime saving value, positive if active, zero if not

The final thing left to do is to convert the tm time to a string using a strftime function and appropriate format specifiers:

```c
#include <stdio.h>
#include <time.h>

int main(void)
{
        time_t mytime = time(NULL);
        struct tm *nowtm;
        char str[70];
        nowtm = localtime(&mytime);
        strftime(str, sizeof str, "%T", nowtm);
        printf("The time is: %s\n", str);
}
```

Output:

```
The time is: 23:02:10
```

The strftime function converts the calendar date/time stored inside the tm structure to a string according to the format specifiers used. Here, we used the %T format specifier, which is the same as the %H:%M:%S format.

To format the obtained date/time as a date only, we can use the %D format specifier. Example:

```c
#include <stdio.h>
#include <time.h>

int main(void)
{
        time_t mytime = time(NULL);
        struct tm *nowtm;
        char str[70];
        nowtm = localtime(&mytime);
        strftime(str, sizeof str, "%D", nowtm);
        printf("The date is: %s\n", str);
}
```

Output:

```
The date is: 11/26/23
```

This example uses the %D format specifier inside the `strftime` function to output only the date part of the obtained date-time. The %D format specifier is equivalent to %m/%d/%y format.

When we populate the `tm` structure, we can access its individual fields. For example, if we need to access and display minutes and seconds as integers, we write:

```
#include <stdio.h>
#include <time.h>

int main(void)
{
    time_t mytime = time(NULL);
    struct tm *nowtm;
    nowtm = localtime(&mytime);
    printf("Minutes and seconds are: %d:%d\n", nowtm->tm_min,
    nowtm->tm_sec);
}
```

Output:

```
Minutes and seconds are: 42:12
```

In this example, we do not convert the obtained date-time to a string using the `strftime` function. We simply use the `tm` structure's fields representing minutes and numbers, called tm_min and tm_sec, and print them out using the `printf` function.

APPENDIX C

Bitwise Operators

So far, we have talked about data in terms of bytes. A *byte* is the smallest addressable region of memory/data storage. We access and manipulate this memory through variables and pointers. One byte can be used to represent the value of a single char variable. Four bytes can be used to represent the value of a single int.

A single byte usually consists of eight smaller parts called *bits*. A bit can have one of two values we symbolically refer to as 0 and 1. A single byte that represents the decimal number 1 can have the following bit representation:

0	0	0	0	0	0	0	1

Figure C-1. *Eight bits representing the decimal number 1*

A single byte representing the decimal value of 10 (usually, depending on the implementation and endianness) has the following bits:

0	0	0	0	1	0	1	0

Figure C-2. *Eight bits representing the decimal number 10*

Bitwise operators allow us to manipulate individual bits of a byte or bytes in several ways. The first bitwise operator we discuss is the bitwise NOT operator ~.

C.1 The Bitwise NOT Operator ~

The bitwise NOT operator ~, also called a *unary complement operator*, returns the result of converting/flipping every bit inside an expression. The operator has the following signature:

```
~expression_of_an_integral_type
```

333

© Slobodan Dmitrović 2024
S. Dmitrović, *Modern C for Absolute Beginners*, https://doi.org/10.1007/979-8-8688-0224-9_50

Every bit's value of 1 becomes 0, and the value of 0 becomes 1. The following example flips the bits of an integer constant 10 and stores the result into our char variable:

```c
#include <stdio.h>

int main(void)
{
    char c = 10;
    printf("The value is: %d\n", c);
    printf("Applying the bitwise ~ operation...\n");
    c = ~10; // bitwise NOT
    printf("The value is: %d\n", c);
}
```

Output:

```
The value is: 10
Applying the bitwise ~ operation...
The value is: -11
```

This example first assigns the value of 10 to our char variable c. Remember, we can assign both numbers and character constants to our chars. The decimal value of 10 is equal to the binary value of 00001010. Now, our byte might look like:

0	0	0	0	1	0	1	0

Figure C-3. *Eight bits representing the decimal value of 10*

Next, we perform the bitwise NOT operation on the integer constant 10 using the ~10 expression and assign the result to our char variable. All the bits are flipped, and the resulting byte now looks like:

1	1	1	1	0	1	0	1

Figure C-4. *Eight bits representing the decimal value of -11*

Our variable c now holds a decimal value of -11, equal to 11110101 in binary.

C.2 Bitwise Shift Operators << and >>

The bitwise shift operators << and >> return the result of shifting the bits of an integral expression to the left/right by N places. The bitwise operands have the following signatures:

integral_expressions << n_places – Shifts bits to the left by
n_places

integral_expressions >> n_places – Shifts bits to the right by
n_places

To shift the bits to the left by four places, we write:

```
#include <stdio.h>

int main(void)
{
    char c = 10;
    printf("The value before the bit shifting is: %d\n", c);
    c = c << 4;
    printf("The value after the bit shifting is: %d\n", c);
}
```

Output:

```
The value before the bit shifting is: 10
The value after the bit shifting is: -96
```

This example assigns the value of decimal 10 to our char variable. Then, it performs the left shift by four places and assigns the result to the same variable. When shifting bits to the left, the vacant bits are filled with zeros. Our byte having a value of 10 before the left shift looked like:

0	0	0	0	1	0	1	0

Figure C-5. *Eight bits representing the number 10*

After the left shift by four places, the byte looks like:

1	0	1	0	0	0	0	0

Figure C-6. *Eight bits representing the value of -96*

The binary value of 10100000 is equal to the decimal value of -96.

If we want to shift the bits to the right by four places, we use the right shift operator >>. Example:

```c
#include <stdio.h>

int main(void)
{
    char c = 10;
    printf("The value before the bit shifting is: %d\n", c);
    c = c >> 4;
    printf("The value after the bit shifting is: %d\n", c);
}
```

Output:

```
The value before the bit shifting is: 10
The value after the bit shifting is: 0
```

In this example, we performed a right shift to the right by four places. In this case, the vacant bits are filled with zeros.

When performing the right shift of a signed integer, the vacant bits are filled either with 0 or with a sign bit, depending on the implementation. An example where we shift the bits of a signed number by four places:

```c
#include <stdio.h>

int main(void)
{
    char c = -10;
    printf("The value before the bit shifting is: %d\n", c);
```

```
    c = c >> 4;
    printf("The value after the bit shifting is: %d\n", c);
}
```

Output:

```
The value before the bit shifting is: -10
The value after the bit shifting is: -1
```

Here, we perform the bit shifting to the right by four places. The vacant bits are filled with a sign bit value (vacant bits are filled with 1), resulting in a decimal value of -1. Before the shift, the byte with a decimal value of -10 looked like:

1	1	1	1	0	1	1	0

Figure C-7. *Eight bits representing the value of -10*

After shifting all bits to the right by four places and filling the vacant bits with 1, the byte looks like:

1	1	1	1	1	1	1	1

Figure C-8. *Eight bits representing the number -1*

Hint   Try shifting the bits of values lesser than -16 to observe results other than -1.

The following example performs the right shift of the unsigned value of 256u to the right by four places:

```
#include <stdio.h>

int main(void)
{
    unsigned x = 256u;
    printf("The value before the bit shifting is: %d\n", x);
```

```
    x = x >> 4;
    printf("The value after the bit shifting is: %d\n", x);
}
```

Output:

```
The value before the bit shifting is: 256
The value after the bit shifting is: 16
```

In this example, we used a variable of an unsigned int type with a decimal value of 256u. Since unsigned can be 4 bytes long, the decimal number of 256 can have the following binary representation:

00000000 00000000 00000001 00000000

After shifting all the bits to the right by four places, the binary value can look like:

00000000 00000000 00000000 00010000

The preceding bits represent the decimal value of 16.

Note   The order of bytes in a multibyte type depends on endianness.

Endianness is the order of bytes (the sequence of bytes) in a multibyte data/memory. The big-endian stores the most significant byte at the beginning. The little-endian stores the most significant bytes at the end of a multibyte memory region.

C.3 The Bitwise AND Operator &

The bitwise AND operator & returns the result of a *logical AND* operation using bits from the left-hand side expression and the corresponding bits from a right-hand side argument. The & operator has the following syntax:

```
left_integral_expression & right_integral_expression
```

If both bits from the left-hand side and the right-hand side expressions are 1, the result will be 1, 0 otherwise. The following table shows the result of a bitwise AND operation:

X	Y	X & Y
1	1	1
0	1	0
1	0	0
0	0	0

An example where we use the logical AND bitwise operator using the 1111 and the 1010 pattern:

```
#include <stdio.h>

int main(void)
{
    unsigned x = 255;
    printf("The value before the bitwise AND: %d\n", x);
    x = x & 0xffff; // 0xffff has the 1111 pattern
    printf("After the bitwise AND using the 1111 mask: %d\n", x);
    unsigned y = 255;
    printf("The value before the bitwise AND: %d\n", y);
    y = y & 0xaaaa; // 0xaaaa has the 1010 pattern
    printf("After the bitwise AND using the 1010 mask: %d\n", y);
}
```

Output:

```
The value before the bitwise AND: 255
After the bitwise AND using the 1111 mask: 255
The value before the bitwise AND: 255
After the bitwise AND using the 1010 mask: 170
```

This example applies the bitwise & operator on its two operands. First, it uses the hexadecimal 0xffff constant as its right-hand side expression. The value of 0xffff corresponds to the 1111 pattern. The result of a 255 & 0xffff expression remains the same as the original 255 value. Next, we perform the bitwise AND operation on bits from y with bits from 0xaaaa hexadecimal constant. The value of 0xaaaa corresponds to the pattern of 1010, and the result of a 255 & 0xaaaa expression is 170 in decimal.

Please note that there are other bitwise operators as well. They are

- Bitwise OR |

- Bitwise exclusive OR ^

- Compound left shift assignment >>=

- Compound right shift assignment <<=

Numeric Limits

The C standard library provides facilities that help us determine numeric limits for various integer and floating-point types.

D.1 Integer Types Limits

The `<limits.h>` header provides useful macros for inspecting the limits of various integer types and objects. Here, we describe a few.

The `CHAR_BIT` macro constant represents the number of bits in a byte. Example:

```c
#include <stdio.h>
#include <limits.h>

int main(void)
{
    printf("The number of bits in a byte: %d\n", CHAR_BIT);
}
```

Output:

```
The number of bits in a byte: 8
```

The `CHAR_MIN` and `CHAR_MAX` macros represent the minimum and maximum values a type `char` can store on our implementation. Example:

```c
#include <stdio.h>
#include <limits.h>

int main(void)
{
    printf("The minimum value a char can store is: %d\n", CHAR_MIN);
```

341

© Slobodan Dmitrović 2024
S. Dmitrović, *Modern C for Absolute Beginners*, https://doi.org/10.1007/979-8-8688-0224-9_51

```
    printf("The maximum value a char can store is: %d\n", CHAR_MAX);
}
```

Output:

```
The minimum value a char can store is: -128
The maximum value a char can store is: 127
```

The INT_MIN and INT_MAX macros represent the minimum and maximum values a type int can hold. Example:

```
#include <stdio.h>
#include <limits.h>

int main(void)
{
    printf("The minimum value an int can store is: %d\n", INT_MIN);
    printf("The maximum value an int can store is: %d\n", INT_MAX);
}
```

Output:

```
The minimum value an int can store is: -2147483648
The maximum value an int can store is: 2147483647
```

Some of the other macro constants declared inside the <limits.h> header are

- LONG_MIN – Minimum value a type long can hold
- LLONG_MIN – Minimum value a type long long can hold
- LONG_MAX – Maximum value a type long can hold
- LLONG_MAX – Maximum value a type long long can hold
- UCHAR_MAX – Maximum value a type unsigned char can hold
- UINT_MAX – Maximum value a type unsigned can hold
- ULONG_MAX – Maximum value a type unsigned long can hold
- ULLONG_MAX – Maximum value a type unsigned long long can hold

D.2 Floating-Point Types Limits

As part of the C standard library, the `<float.h>` header defines several macros representing minimum and maximum values for floating-point types.

The FLT_MIN macro represents the minimum, positive value of type float. Example:

```
#include <stdio.h>
#include <float.h>

int main(void)
{
    printf("The minimum, positive value for a float is: %e\n", FLT_MIN);
}
```

Output:

```
The minimum, positive value for a float is: 1.175494e-38
```

In this example, we used the %e format specifier, which converts the floating-point value to an exponent decimal (scientific) representation.

The FLT_MAX macro represents the maximum value for type float. Example:

```
#include <stdio.h>
#include <float.h>

int main(void)
{
    printf("The maximum value for a float is: %f\n", FLT_MAX);
}
```

Output:

```
The maximum value for a float is:
340282346638528859811704183484516925440.000000
```

Another essential macro is the FLT_EPSILON constant, representing the difference between 1.0 and the next number that can be represented using type float. Example:

```
#include <stdio.h>
#include <float.h>

int main(void)
{
    float f = 1.0f;
    printf("The value of f is: %e\n", f);
    printf("The next representable number is larger by: %e\n",
    FLT_EPSILON);
}
```

Output:

```
The value of f is: 1.000000e+00
The next representable number is larger by: 1.192093e-07
```

Other floating-point macro constants are

- DBL_EPSILON – The difference between 1.0 and the next number that can be represented using the type double

- LDBL_EPSILON – The difference between 1.0 and the next number that can be represented using the type long double

- DBL_MIN – Minimum, positive value for type double

- LDBL_MIN – Minimum, positive value for type long double

- DBL_MAX – Maximum value for type double

- LDBL_MAX – Maximum value for type long double

APPENDIX E

Summary and Advice

Dear reader, congratulations on finishing reading this book. At this point, you should be sufficiently familiar with the C language and C standard library essentials.

Even after many decades, the C programming language still grows strong. Where is C used in the real world? Major operating systems were written in C. Our machines are packed with different hardware whose software was written in C. Large industrial facilities are controlled by machines that run on software written in C. A great deal of embedded development relies on C. So, being a C developer is a good career choice.

E.1 What to Learn Next?

Once we write our program, we want to be able to step through the code and inspect all the values. This is called *debugging*. Learn about debugging using *GDB* if on Linux or using a built-in debugger in Visual Studio.

Learn about data structures and algorithms and how they can be implemented in C.

When we have a large project consisting of multiple files, we want to compile them by invoking an underlying build system. Learn about the build systems such as *Make* and *CMake*.

Software projects are managed using the so-called *source control* or *version control* software. This software allows us to manage and control changes to our source code. We commit the source code to the repository, make changes, and revert the code when needed. Learn about version control software such as *Git*, *Subversion*, and others.

Explore existing C projects found on GitHub as well as other open source projects written in C.

© Slobodan Dmitrović 2024
S. Dmitrović, *Modern C for Absolute Beginners*, https://doi.org/10.1007/979-8-8688-0224-9_52

E.2 Online References

There is a user-maintained, well-written online C reference at

```
https://en.cppreference.com/w/c
```

The C language and standard library drafts can be downloaded as PDF documents from

```
https://en.cppreference.com/w/c/links
```

Linux manual pages are available at

```
https://linux.die.net/man/
```

And

```
https://man7.org/linux/man-pages/
```

E.3 Other C Books

For more C books, refer to a curated list of C books on Stack Overflow:

```
https://stackoverflow.com/questions/562303/the-definitive-c-book-
guide-and-list
```

E.4 Advice

C is a straightforward, procedural, and relatively concise language. It is a language that efficiently maps to hardware and gives us immense control over the machine. The following is some advice that might help you further advance your C knowledge.

Be sure to make the distinction between C and C++ as they are two completely different languages.

But above all, enjoy programming in C, as the world of C programming is a rewarding and exciting place to be in.

Index

© Slobodan Dmitrović 2024
S. Dmitrović, *Modern C for Absolute Beginners*, https://doi.org/10.1007/979-8-8688-0224-9

Printed in the United States
by Baker & Taylor Publisher Services